PIPPA FUNNELL

TRAINING the YOUNG HORSE

Schooling for Success

WRITTEN WITH KATE GREEN

PHOTOGRAPHY BY KIT HOUGHTON

David & Charles

Contents

Funnell Vision

Bringing on a young horse is, to my mind, one of the most fascinating and satisfying projects you can undertake, and it has often given me more pleasure to produce a youngster from the beginning than it has been to win on a 'made' horse.

I get as much satisfaction from producing a young horse and getting it to its first competition as I do riding at top level. At the start of a young horse's career there are no expectations, so I feel that everything that goes right is a bonus. I don't just view training as a way to guarantee success, but as a means of ensuring an easier and more pleasant ride. Therefore, this book is not necessarily for riders who intend to compete; it is for all those who wish to produce a young horse that is safe, well mannered, happy and confident – in short, an enjoyable ride.

I have always been involved with young horses and have learned to produce them myself, even as a small child – my first pony, Pepsi, who came from the Brooks-Ward family, was an eight-year-old rather than the traditional elderly Shetland.

The opportunity I've had to lead a life with horses I owe to my parents Jenny and George Nolan; they sacrificed a lot to make it all possible and have always supported me. Although my mother never competed at international level, she instilled in me very high standards of stable management and turnout which, thirty-two years on, still stand me in good stead. I was fortunate, though, not to be pushed by her; I very much learned what I know today through having fun with my ponies, whether it was hunting, playing cowboys and Indians, or going to Pony Club.

It was my mother's friendship with Ruth McMullen which proved the opening to my career with horses: I was seven when I got Flighty, a three-year-old 12.2hh, from her. He was nappy and I was always getting bucked off – he trod on my fingers one day – but I loved him, and I learned right from the start that you can't let a young horse get away with behaving badly. You have to deal with problems as they occur, because if you put them off, they will multiply.

Flighty was followed by Jeremy Fisher, a five-year-old 13.2hh, who used to twist so badly when jumping verticals that he would jump me off. As a child, you tend not to think technically, but with Jeremy I soon learned

One of the highlights: (*page 6*) Supreme Rock at Luhmuhlen in 1999

Sir Barnaby: (*left*) The dressage phase in 1990, on our way to my best Badminton placing – 5th

that if I didn't place him correctly at a fence, I'd fall off. And he taught me a lot about patience; if I lost my temper with him it would put him back two weeks in progress, and at that early age I *did* tend to lose my temper!

Then, when I was a teenager, came my first horse, Sir Barnaby, probably still one of my best known event horses. He was a five-year-old, and had been bought for meat money by Ruth McMullen, who was to become my trainer and who had decided he was the horse for me.

I'll never forget my first day with Barnaby. Jeremy Fisher's new owners had arrived and I was in floods of tears as he left. I turned away to go and see my new horse and found him standing on his hindlegs with his forelegs hanging over the stable partition, trying to see where his nextdoor neighbour had gone! He looked absolutely terrifying, and I felt very lost without my pony.

Sir Barnaby: He had more heart than any horse I have ever ridden. It was his will to succeed rather than his ability that made him such a good horse

By the end of my first week with Barnaby I was in despair and not at all sure I would cope. He was naughty on the roads, whipping around at the slightest thing; he jumped fences from a standstill because he just had to have a look at what might be on the other side; and he would muck about on the flat, shooting off and bucking. One day he spooked at some milk crates and hit a car. Luckily he wasn't injured, but it scared me and made me realise that I had to sort him out. From then on I learned to be one step ahead of him. You couldn't fight him, so it was a case of riding forwards and being firm rather than tentative.

But even though I sometimes felt I really hated him, especially after a dressage test, he was still a winner. My experience with young ponies had taught me to stick on, and although Barnaby was cheeky, he wasn't nasty and he had an incredible sense of self-preservation. I have since ridden young horses without that quality, and they aren't such good news.

I have always been hungry and competitive for success, and even then, would analyse my performance, working out what could be improved. Barnaby was a good example of how a cheeky young horse can be worth persevering with, and I have since learned that it isn't necessarily the horses who have the most talent that get to the top; it's the ones with the biggest heart.

I remember being entered for a junior trial (for the British junior

The Tourmaline Rose: (*right*) Winning the first Eventer's Grand Prix at Hickstead, a new competition over the Derby fences, in 1998, an event we won on two more occasions

Bits and Pieces: (*below*) A horse that wasn't really made for top level competition but who thrived on jumping. He never gave me a feeling of scope at home, but he was transformed at a major event, always looking for the next fence and making the big tracks seem easy, here at the Cottesmore Leap, Burghley, in 1994

European Championships: (*right*) The hard
work paid off and all the elements came
together in 1999. My gratitude to
Supreme Rock when he won me my first
individual title made me realise how
special our partnership had become

Winning team: (*above*) Emma Pitt,
Rocky's owner (*left*), with her sister, Marie
Claire (*right*) and in the centre Zanie
Tanswell, my head girl, who does so
much work behind the scenes. I owe
much of my success to my girls

Supreme Rock ('Rocky'): (*left*) Rocky en route to winning the Chatsworth CIC in 2000, which was some compensation for missing Badminton as part of our Olympic preparation

Grand Prix success again: (*right*) Anne Burnet's The Tourmaline Rose, whom I started riding as a 4-year-old, wins her second Eventer's Grand Prix. She is one of the spookiest horses I've ridden, but one of the most careful jumpers

Sydney 2000: (*below*) Rocky performing one of his best ever tests at the Olympic Games. As well as his super temperament he has *such* expressive paces. He is seen here performing shoulder in

eventing team) and went to Ruth McMullen for lessons. The dressage test for the trial involved entering the arena at canter, but Ruth wouldn't let me out of a walk for five days! I was in tears, thinking that at this rate we had no hope of achieving anything; but Ruth said that if I couldn't get it right at the walk I wouldn't get any further, and she was right.

I spent eight busy years working for Ruth in her Norfolk yard, where I gained the experience of riding all sorts of young horses. Ruth wasn't one for rushing a horse; she was such a perfectionist, and went into so much detail that I never stopped learning. She was a great horsewoman, and could take on really difficult horses and effect such a transformation that people would think she had doped them! She never lost her temper – unless it was with people, if she caught anyone getting after a horse – and she believed that you could change any horse through work at home. Ruth's ethic was that the horse itself will teach you more than anybody

Team result: (*left*) Celebrating Britain's Olympic silver medal with Ian Stark, Jeanette Breakwell and Leslie Law

European Championship dressage: (*below*) An unusual photo of Rocky at Pau, with all four feet off the ground

else. There was a huge variety of horses to ride there, from ponies to racehorses and it was this invaluable experience that Ruth was able to offer me, together with all her help, that gave me the chance to pursue my passion.

Ruth has always maintained that eighty-five per cent of a horse's problems come from the jockey, and this is why I have tried to make it clear in this book that the rider has a huge responsibility towards the development of the young horse.

I tend to be, perhaps, a bit on the soft side and as a result, I have probably wasted a lot of time over the years being a bit soppy with my horses, but I have always believed that the relationship between horse and rider has to be a real partnership: you've got to be friends, not working against each other. I like to spend a lot of time in the stable with youngsters, just fiddling around with them, and although this book does not cover the very early stages with foals and yearlings, I am convinced that the more handling they receive early on, the easier they will be to break in and the better mannered they will be.

One of the things that attracted me to my husband William, who is an international show jumper, was the way he seemed to have a rapport with his horses. I certainly couldn't have married anyone who was rough with a horse. William's riding background has, however, been more commercial than mine; he is sent young horses from all over England and Europe to break in and school on, and he also sells several. He has good hands, is laid back and has incredible patience, but in the nicest possible way, he doesn't stand any nonsense, either.

William has taught me that I used to help my younger horses too much when jumping; he believes that the rider should let them learn from their own mistakes. I tended to over-correct my young horses, and tried to manufacture their canter too much instead of letting them find their own self-carriage and allowing them to go more naturally. As a result, I have realised that very often the rider need not work so hard, and should not interfere too much with the horse. It must be remembered that the rider should never want to dominate the horse: it should be allowed to retain its natural personality, for horses are all individuals. Letting them have the occasional buck and play without becoming dangerous is an important way of maintaining their enjoyment of life. As mere riders, we can't compete with a

European Championship cross country: (*right*) I had the sort of ride you dream about, though on finishing the feeling of relief was overwhelming

In the medals: (*below*) Yet again, Rocky proves his consistent generosity

horse's strength, so educating a young horse is, to a large extent, actually a series of 'mind games'.

This book covers the process of training a young horse, from handling and backing a two- or three-year-old, through training and preparing a horse for its first competitions, and the progression from there, and is based on my own personal methods, which I have learned through experience and with much help, and according to the facilities available to me. I may not do everything 'by the book', but I want to emphasise that every horse is different and needs an individual approach. I also want to make it clear that no one should think that by just reading a book they can expect to produce a young horse: it is essential to ask for help.

I am also a firm believer in being realistic. In my experience, those horses who are really difficult to handle as youngsters and who don't seem to want to learn are never going to make ideal mounts, for there is a difference between mere naughtiness and being impossible. Many of the brilliant horses you see at competitions have perhaps been less than easy to produce, but they will all have been willing to learn.

Although every horse can be improved to a certain extent, if you have used all the right methods and still find that he doesn't want to be trained, then don't be ashamed to give up and pass him to someone else. The bottom line is that a horse must be trainable, and if he is that impossible, he probably will never be an obliging, reliable ride.

Team training: (*left*) Having some fun on Anne Burnet's Jurassic Rising during team training at Eddy Stibbe's Waresley Park. Jurassic Rising was one of the four horses I had on the long list for the European Championships at Pau in 2001

Supporters' club: (*top right*) My parents, Jenny and George Nolan, and brother Tim whose support has always been invaluable

European Champions: (*right*) Rocky on his way to a record back-to-back victory at the European Championships in Pau, 2001. He made up too much ground in the combination, crashing through the last element, in the show jumping. At that point I realised what a fine line there is between success and failure!

MAJOR RESULTS

1986
➤ Team bronze at Junior European Championships (Airborne ll), 5th Chatsworth (Sir Barnaby)

'87
➤ Individual gold, Young Rider European Championships (Sir Barnaby)

'88
➤ Completed Badminton, 8th and team gold at Young Rider Europeans (Sir Barnaby)

'89
➤ Individual and team silver medals, Young Rider Europeans (Sir Barnaby)

1990
➤ 5th Badminton (Sir Barnaby), 3rd British Intermediate Championships (Metronome), 2nd British Open Championships (Sir Barnaby)

'91
➤ 10th Breda (Heron's Flight), 13th Bramham (Metronome), 1st Luhmuhlen, 2nd British Open, 4th Burghley (Sir Barnaby)

'92
➤ Completed Badminton (Sir Barnaby), 3rd Windsor (Cartoon), 1st Bramham (Metronome), 7th Bramham (Heron's Flight), 1st British Open (Sir Barnaby), 3rd Blenheim (Cartoon), 16th Burghley (Heron's Flight)

'93
➤ 2nd Windsor (Merry Gambler), 1st Blenheim (Metronome), 16th Burghley (Cartoon)

'95
➤ 1st Windsor (Designer Tramp), 1st and 8th Blenheim (Bits And Pieces and The Imposter)

'96
➤ 1st Windsor (Marshland Rubio), 4th Burghley (Bits And Pieces), 1st & 4th Achselschwang (Rainbow Magic and Supreme Rock)

'97
➤ 2nd Punchestown (Designer Tramp), 9th Badminton and competed as individual for Open European Championships (Bits And Pieces)

'98
➤ 1st Hickstead Eventer's Grand Prix (The Tourmaline Rose), 4th British Open, 5th Blenheim (Rainbow Magic)

'99
➤ 6th Badminton (Supreme Rock), 1st Punchestown (General Salute), team and individual gold medals at European Championships (Supreme Rock), 4th Achselschwang (General Salute), 4th Le Lion d'Angers (Jurassic Rising)

2000
➤ 1st Chatsworth (Supreme Rock), 4th Punchestown (Primmore's Pride), 4th and 7th Bramham (Jurassic Rising and Cornerman), 2nd and 4th Burgie (Viceroy and Burke's Boy), 1st Hickstead Eventer's Grand Prix (The Tourmaline Rose), Olympic team silver, Sydney 2000 (Supreme Rock), 1st Le Lion d'Angers (Primmore's Pride)

'01
➤ 2nd Saumur (Viceroy), 1st Burgie (Teddy Twilight), 4th Burgie (Walk On Star), 11th Luhmuhlen (Jurassic Rising), 1st Hickstead Eventer's Grand Prix (The Tourmaline Rose), 1st Scottish Open Championships (Supreme Rock), 8th Hickstead Speed Derby (The Tourmaline Rose), 5th Burghley (Cornerman), 4th Blenheim (Primmore's Pride), 1st Windsor (Burke's Boy), team and individual gold medals at European Championships Pau (Supreme Rock)

Finding the right horse

In order for me to want to buy a horse, I have to feel so excited about it that I can't wait to get it home and start riding it. Generally, though, rather than choosing my own horses, I have been lucky to have been sent many good horses to ride – though I have still tried to be realistic when assessing these horses, as their owners need to know how suitable they are for the job they want them to do.

The horse's conformation is important in all branches of equestrianism because if its physical make-up is faulty in some way, then this will put more strain on other parts of the body and make certain types of work more difficult for it; moreover serious conformation defects often end in lameness and it is important to think carefully about what you are really hoping to do with your young horse. Having said that, few horses are perfect. I have ridden horses with minor conformation defects and these have not caused any major problem.

For me, quality is another important factor. For eventing I prefer a full Thoroughbred or one that is seven-eighths bred for its 'cruising gear', speed, stamina and courage; but you would still be advised to go for plenty of blood in a jumping or dressage horse: a horse that lacks quality will always be having to work in its 'top gear' and this will eventually lead to physical problems – strains, sprains and lameness.

First impressions

The very first impression of a horse can be the deciding factor for me. I want to see what its natural attitude to life is – preferably interested and bold – how kind its eye is, and how freely it walks out of the stable. I love big eyes and ears, a keen, interested outlook, and I would not be attracted to a horse who comes out of the stable looking 'pottery' or disinterested.

Many riders use expressions like 'fitting in the square box', 'a leg at each corner' or 'filling the eye' to describe a horse who is compact and pleasing to look at and looks as if it will fit in an imaginary square box. But often with young horses one has to use one's imagination; many do not look impressive until they are saddled up and working, and with others you have to visualise how they are going to develop. Teddy Twilight, who was bought by Ian and Janet McIntyre as a four-year-old and sent to me, looked rather a runt at 15.2hh, but with work and natural maturity he is now a strapping 16.1hh, and at seven has won his first three-day event.

It is important to me that the horse is in proportion, with bone that fits its body. I would be happy with a light-boned horse as long as it was a light Thoroughbred in build – small bones and a big body on top will lead to problems of leg strain; big limbs and a light body indicate common blood.

A pet hate of mine is horses who are long in the pastern because this could put a strain on the tendons and, therefore, lead to soundness problems. I dislike a horse who is back at the knee (where the knee appears to be behind the rest of the leg), as this could also lead to strained tendons, and any sign of wear around the joints – swelling, or joints of unequal size or appearance – in a young horse would also put me off.

Most of the horses I have had who have ended up with soundness problems have been weak behind. This is because their front ends must work extra hard in order to compensate for this weakness, and this can eventually cause back and/or tendon strain. I believe that tendon injuries are more frequently caused from the cumulative effect in horses who cannot and do not work properly from behind, than from landing awkwardly over a fence or pulling out of deep mud.

A ewe neck (one that seems to dip in the middle) would not worry me, but I do like the neck to appear to come out of the 'right socket', by which I mean coming high out of the shoulder in an uphill, rounded shape. A horse whose neck is attached low to its body will tend to be naturally very on its forehand.

The shoulder should be strong and sloping from clearly defined withers for optimum scope and good movement, and the chest reasonably wide – this promises enough room for heart and lungs to function well. Also, if the front legs look as if they come out of the same hole there is a greater risk of injury through brushing.

I also look out for the way the horse carries its back end. Long, short, dipped or roach (convex) backs are not an issue for me, as long as the horse's hindlegs look to be properly underneath his body and not stretched out behind him, because that is likely to indicate a lack of power in the back end.

'No foot, no horse' is another very true old adage, so I have a good look at each hoof, which should be well shaped, not too shallow, flat and not too boxy. Whenever I have had reservations about a horse's feet in the past, they have nearly always been dogged with soundness problems, making corrective shoeing essential.

I always ask for the horse to be walked and trotted up for me so that I can see how evenly he places his feet, and to see whether he has a natural, swinging length of stride or whether he 'pokes' along. The latter is hard to improve and might affect your chances of earning decent dressage marks or winning a showing class and it can indicate lack of scope.

I wouldn't be put off by a horse who dishes – Supreme Rock, my Olympic ride, is a very impressive horse when stood up and is a lovely big mover, but if you stand directly behind or in front of him when he trots up, you will see that his legs go everywhere. However, when his feet hit the ground they do so evenly, and that's what is important.

First impressions: (*left*)
To me there's a certain look about a horse that indicates his qualities – you can see the generosity in a good horse's expression. You can see from his eye the kindness and the will to please. If he loves his job you can read it in his face

Matter of Fact: (*page 18*)
Owned by Sarah Jewson, this young horse shows he is still rather green, fumbling behind as we go into the water, but the expressions on both our faces are a clear sign that we are having fun

The will to win

My three best horses to date are Sir Barnaby, Bits And Pieces and Supreme Rock, none of whom was possessed with the most natural ability – although Barnaby and Rocky both have good conformation – and this leads on to what is, for me, the most important issue: the heart and the brain. This you cannot judge from a one-off inspection but plays a vital role in how far up the ladder of success a horse may be capable of rising.

All great horses, whether top racehorses, eventers, show jumpers or dressage horses, have had one thing in common: the will to win and the urge to keep trying for you, working out what you want from them and doing their utmost to please.

You can do as much training as you like to make a horse stronger and to improve its way of going, but it is the heart and its generosity that will separate the good horses from the top ones.

I believe you can draw a comparison between human and equine athletes, for even if several top sprinters all have the same physical attributes and methods of training, what separates the best from the rest is character and mental attitude.

Winning ways: Supreme Rock at the Sydney Olympics, 2000; a horse that really responds to the atmosphere of a big occasion and performs to the best of his ability

Best of All

A horse who took a long time to grow on me. Owned by Sarah Jewson, this 16.3hh bay gelding was bred, by Nicky Stephens, to win Badminton! He is by the leading sports horse sire Sportsnight out of Twist or Bust, a mare from a distinguished eventing line.

'Muffin' (the mule!) came to me as a four-year-old and took every opportunity to use his strength and size against me. He wasn't mature enough to compete in the spring season of his five-year-old year so Tanya Liddle

started him that autumn while I was away in Sydney.

When 'Muffin' returned as a six-year-old my opinion was the same: that he was a thug and used his strength to avoid work. But because Sarah longed for me to compete him, I persevered and in the ensuing months he made such a huge improvement and showed such a wonderful attitude at his first competitions, where he was placed consistently, that my initial feelings have completely dispersed.

Good sloping shoulder with withers well set back, giving good length of rein and promising scope and a long stride.

One of the main points to look for is a good length from the hip bone to the point of the hock, for strength and scope.

A line drawn straight across the widest part of the quarters should be a good length, indicating powerful hind quarters.

The length from the elbow to the knee should be roughly the same as from the knee to the foot, for strength in the limb.

Matter of Fact

I have never come across a horse with such a willing nature. A 16.1hh gelding from a family of Irish sport horses that can be traced back to King Of Diamonds, Sarah Jewson sent 'Matty' to me as a freshly broken four-year-old.

He politely did everything asked of him and I haven't come across a bad bone in his body. He has been introduced to eventing quietly and been placed a few times. As yet I can't tell how far up the ladder he will go but, with his attitude both in and out of the stable, he is a lovely character to have around.

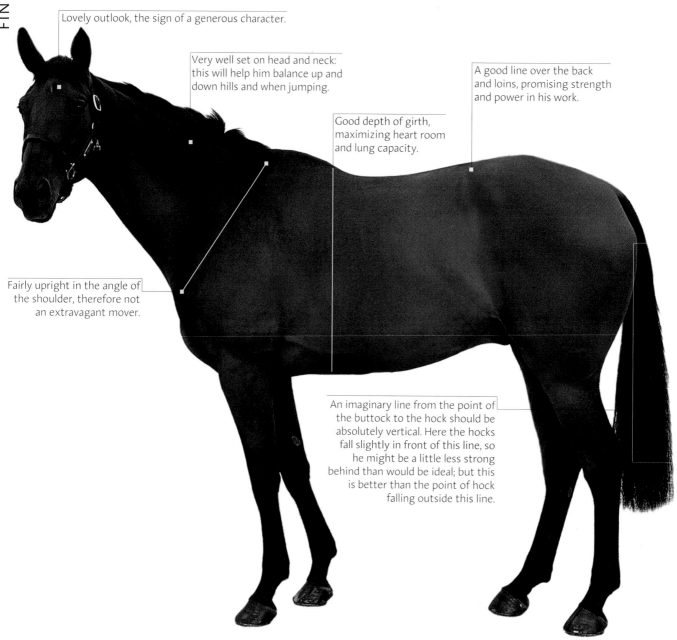

Lovely outlook, the sign of a generous character.

Very well set on head and neck: this will help him balance up and down hills and when jumping.

A good line over the back and loins, promising strength and power in his work.

Good depth of girth, maximizing heart room and lung capacity.

Fairly upright in the angle of the shoulder, therefore not an extravagant mover.

An imaginary line from the point of the buttock to the hock should be absolutely vertical. Here the hocks fall slightly in front of this line, so he might be a little less strong behind than would be ideal; but this is better than the point of hock falling outside this line.

Teddy Twilight

Owned by Janet and Ian McIntyre, this horse, thought to be by Edmund Burke (but if he *is* by him, then my father is Linford Christie!), should have been christened Tiger Ted. He has a huge personality and, at 16.1hh, is built like a power-packed little athlete. He has the best hind legs of all my horses. A very good example of a horse that fits the 'square box'.

He is always in trouble, whether it is trying to get his rugs off or kicking continuously in the lorry because he doesn't like his travel boots (we have to travel him with bare back legs now). When on the horse-walker he pushes it so that the poor horse in front has to speed up!

He has got a lot of ability and won his first three-day event, but I am always struggling to cope with his short attention span.

Super length from the hip to the point of the hock.

Very cheeky face, showing how naughty he can be, but he does have a lovely outlook.

Good heart room.

Very well set on forelimb with good bone, which should help him stay sound throughout an active jumping career. He has super limbs and stands very much with 'a leg in each corner'.

Strong second thigh. Excellent in pastern and fetlock: joint looks strong – no lumps or swellings – and angle of pastern is good, neither too upright nor too sloping.

Burke's Boy

Another Irish-bred advanced horse by Edmund Burke, 'Paddy', who is also owned by the McIntyres, came to me late in his career as a 10-year-old. He had previously been hunted by Stuart Campbell in Leicestershire and had evented for a season. I suggested to the McIntyres that they buy him purely because he was by Edmund Burke and the moment I sat on him I realised he shared so many similarities with Supreme Rock that I felt he was worth taking a chance with, despite his advanced age. Interestingly, Paddy, who has the same big movement and scope over a fence as Rocky, also has similar weaknesses, mainly in his canter work. This is partly due to him being slightly long in the back – one would describe him as fitting in a rectangular box rather than a square one – and he therefore finds it difficult to engage the back end.

Mentally, he has had an attitude problem and I am continuously having to work on keeping him forward and in front of the leg. He is idle and 'saves some for himself' but he is improving as he becomes physically stronger from the training.

Straight in the back, so you tend to feel you are sitting on top of him rather than 'into' him.

Slightly long in the back, so he finds it difficult to engage properly from behind: this compromises the amount of power he can produce.

Forelimbs are set on well.

A little straight in the hind leg, so he finds it difficult to push in the walk and canter.

Viceroy

An advanced stallion, 'Leroy' was bred 'by accident' when his American show jumper sire, VIP, escaped during Hickstead and jumped in with one of Sue Bunn's Thoroughbred mares. He first came to us as a four-year-old and was show jumped by my husband William, only changing to eventing when he was eight.

Leroy has an amazing temperament and, apart from being tempted by a mare in season, you forget he is a stallion. I wouldn't normally take on a stallion because their testosterone levels can make them a nuisance and, even with a sensible one like Leroy, you must be always aware that they are unpredictable.

Another feature of his is that he takes a long time to get fit, as I discovered on his first four-star run.

I only took Leroy on as a 'fun' horse, but he has amazed me with his consistency. One of the greatest buzzes of pleasure during my whole career was his behaviour when he became top stallion at the Sport Horse Breeders (GB) grading in 2001. During the loose jumping, instead of galloping around like the other stallions in the class, he would return to my side and stand as quietly as a lamb. I think it may have been this display of temperament which so impressed the judges.

Head and neck set on well, though his neck lacks length; he tends to look overbent when he is tense, which can lose marks.

Good topline: nicely rounded, back neither too long nor too short, blends into quarters in an uninterrupted line – promises power and athleticism.

Good depth of girth: indicates plenty of room for the working of heart and lungs.

Over-developed muscle on the underside means that he will all too readily shorten his neck.

Wonderful limbs and feet. His unblemished legs mean that you would never realise the work he's done.

Cornerman

A well-bred 16.2hh advanced gelding by Neltino out of a Lord Gayle mare, this horse oozes Thoroughbred class and quality. A wonderful cross-country horse with a great gallop, he is an ideal stamp of event horse made for four-star level. Owned and bred by Susie Cranston, 'Charlie' did not come to me until he was eight and he needed a huge amount of work. The main problem was that he had been allowed to move crookedly and, as a result, he finds flatwork hard. My first impression was that he was lazy, but when the lack of straightness had been corrected, he automatically became much more forward.

He is very soppy in the stable which is lovely, but he is sensitive (my head girl Zanie Tanswell calls him 'Precious') and in the wrong hands he would be a worrier.

Excellent line head to wither: head is well set on to neck, and neck to body, in a rounded 'uphill' shape that promises an easy, balanced, 'uphill' way of going. As a model, apart from being one of the nicest looking horses I have, he is also the most conformationally correct.

Lovely Thoroughbred head: calm, generous eye; ears clean and alert; projects quality and intelligence.

Super length in the angles of the back leg, promising plenty of scope and speed.

You could say that he needs slightly more bone.

Quite long in the pastern. Although he undeniably oozes Thoroughbred quality, any faults you could pick in his conformation can be found from his knees downwards.

Typical Thoroughbred feet, quite flat and shallow, that need plenty of care.

Primmore's Pride

Another horse ideally bred for eventing, being by Mark Todd's advanced-level Thoroughbred Mayhill, out of Roger and Joanna Day's Primmore Hill, who was consistent at four-star level. Denise and Roger Lincoln bought him as a foal and from the first moment 'Kiri' has oozed star potential. He has been so successful at two and three-star level, that I can't wait to see what happens as he heads for the top.

He has real ability over a fence and, for his size (17.1hh) and 'legginess', he is quick-brained and agile so that he is capable of getting himself out of trouble. Kiri was straightforward to break, but he developed a bit of an 'attitude' where he would often have to be asked to do something more than once. If he had been allowed to get his own way at an early stage, he would not be the horse he is today.

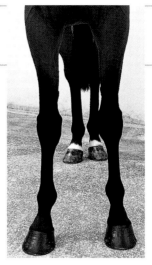

Primmore's Pride is rather angular and narrow, as this front view shows, which could make him prone to 'brushing'

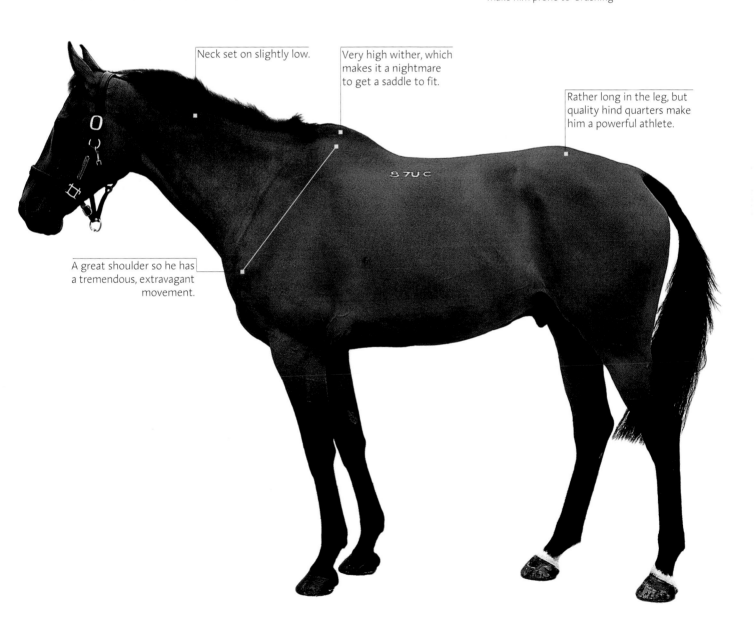

Neck set on slightly low.

Very high wither, which makes it a nightmare to get a saddle to fit.

Rather long in the leg, but quality hind quarters make him a powerful athlete.

A great shoulder so he has a tremendous, extravagant movement.

Supreme Rock

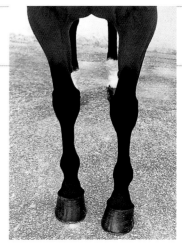

The only horse ever to have won two individual European titles, but when I first rode him I felt he was too laid back and slow-brained to be a champion. Owned by the Lewthwaite and Pitt families, 'Rocky', 16.3hh and Irish-bred, by Edmund Burke out of Rineen Classic, is a good example of a horse whose weaknesses I have had to accept.

Despite his scope, Rocky found it difficult to naturally shorten his stride and jump from a deep spot. For many years I tried to cure this, but when I accepted it and adjusted my riding style, it was a turning point. I had to learn to be accurate and give him more room on take-off. This shows how a rider mustn't dishearten a horse by focussing on their weaknesses, but give them confidence by working on their strengths.

Another major factor in Rocky's success is how the atmosphere at big events helps him to 'up his game'. He really does rise to the big occasion.

Rocky has a slight conformational fault, shown here, where he turns in his toe. This makes him 'throw a leg' a little, but by the time his foot strikes the ground it is balanced and level. Good shoeing is important in dealing with this quirk

Lovely big ears.

Head and neck set on really well to shoulder.

His back is such that you can sit 'into' him, not just on top of him.

Good depth for heart room and lung capacity.

Super across the loins which has developed with correct work.

Good shoulder which means he has an amazing walk and big movement.

Very well developed second thighs, and a generally powerful 'back end'.

Good strong feet.

Sir Barnaby

Words cannot describe how special this horse is. He's an amazing little (16.1hh) horse by a Thoroughbred sire out of a pony mare, and it would be really interesting to find out what would happen if I was riding Barnaby in competition today, to see whether we would have still reached the same heights, as much of his career was taken up by Pony Club events. Because he was my only horse then, I competed him week in and week out on all types of going and always to win, which proves what an incredibly sound horse he is.

This is obviously a picture of a now elderly (24-year-old) horse, but you can see what wonderful conformation he has. I would be happy to see a five-year-old with clean legs like this, and Barnaby has done 16 three-day events!

It was his brain and attitude which made him a winner. He taught me more than any other horse because he was so intelligent and sensitive to the rider's weight – if I didn't get it right, it was an excuse to misbehave. You just had to maintain straightness and true connection to keep him focused and listening.

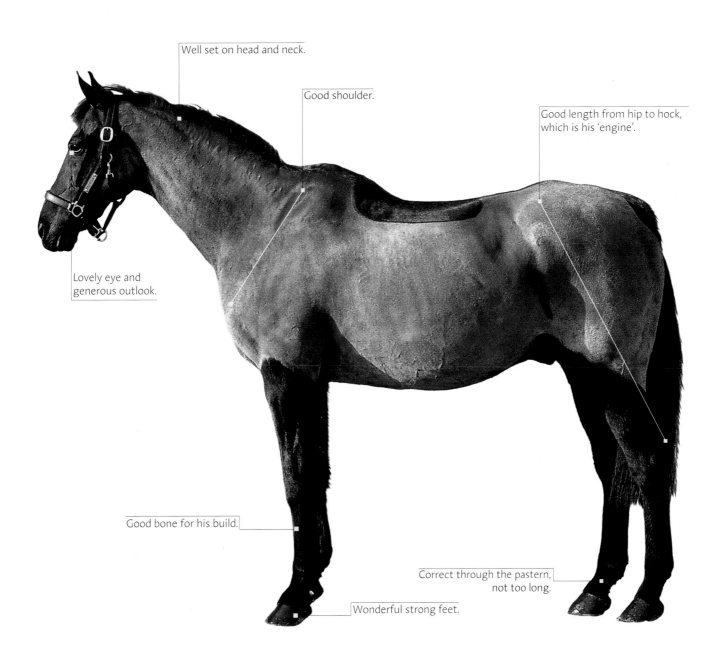

Well set on head and neck.

Good shoulder.

Good length from hip to hock, which is his 'engine'.

Lovely eye and generous outlook.

Good bone for his build.

Correct through the pastern, not too long.

Wonderful strong feet.

Giving your youngster the best start

One of the most fascinating aspects of producing young horses is how quickly, with the right handling, they can change in their temperament, growing in confidence and learning to trust their owner. Some horses change quickly; with others it's a longer process. This is partly due to the way they have been handled as foals and, therefore, how much they are used to human contact by the time they arrive with me; and in part it is due to their own courage and personality.

I've been fortunate enough to have been sent all sorts of youngsters, from unbroken ones over from the wilds of Ireland to people's home-breds who have been well handled by them from day one. During the years I spent working for Ruth McMullen I had the opportunity to deal with a great many youngsters, most of which Ruth had bred herself. She had the most wonderful calm, firm manner with a horse, so that with a lot of these babies you could put your weight on their back even before they were 'officially' broken as they had so much trust in the people around them. I am a firm believer that it is the responsibility of us riders to promote the efforts of breeders by doing a good job in breaking and producing their young horses. The initial financial outlay has come from the breeder, and without them none of us would have decent horses to ride.

Education for the two-year-old

In-hand showing is not a necessity for the yearling or two-year-old, but it is undoubtedly a great education for him – and for you! – if you can put the time to it. Even if you have no pretensions to winning, it is nevertheless important that the youngster is well presented: neat and tidy, with well brushed coat, pulled mane and oiled hooves; he must lead obediently in hand; he must respond readily to voice commands; and he should learn generally to respect you, and anyone else – probably the judge or steward – who might come up and touch him.

This means that in preparing him for the showring he will be well used to being groomed, and having his feet picked out, and perhaps trimmed by the farrier; he will have learned to tie up; and he will have to practise going in and out of the trailer or lorry. It also means that you make the effort to handle him, and get him used to people and yard routine, rather than just leaving him in the field, wild and unmannerly, until it is time for him to be broken in – which could then be traumatic. If he has had this experience, by the time he is three the progression to breaking in and being ridden will be easy for him, just the next step in his education, with no stress or trauma.

If the two-year-old is strong he may need to be shown in a bridle, in which case he will have to get used to a bit – again, a valuable lesson, and another step towards an easy breaking in when he is three. You must take great care if you do this, however, as his mouth and skin are extremely soft and sensitive at this age: use a nylon or rubber straightbar, loose-ring bit, with a mouthpiece that is not too thick. And before you go to your show, be sure that he is quite familiar with this object in his mouth, and that he has had plenty of opportunity to get used to it. To begin with, let him wear it for half an hour or so in the stable, and do this every day for five or six days; then put the headcollar over the top of the bridle and lead him from the headcollar, but with the bit still in his mouth (obviously!). Eventually you may lead him gently from the bit, using a brass or leather coupling.

In preparation for the showring he must learn to walk and trot out confidently, and to stand square. This in itself is a significant lesson, because he must leave the other horses and trot away from them calmly and willingly without a backward glance and not a thought of being nappy. Choose a quiet local event for your youngster's first outing – a large county show with its noisy, bustling activity might be too much for his cool! But even a small show is an important step in his education: he is bound to find it all really exciting, but must learn to behave himself in spite of all the distractions.

All in all, by the time he gets to his first ridden show or event as a four- or five-year-old, he will be quite the old hand!

SHOWING IN HAND: The two-year-old must learn to trot up with panache and presence – this is important, because it is the only time his action is demonstrated individually whilst he is in the ring

The first day

It certainly does make life easier if the youngster has been handled from the start, because it is generally more sure of itself and used to having people around. It is also, however, pretty obvious when a youngster has been spoilt and allowed to become unruly – the equine version of the spoilt kid who needs disciplining.

There tend to be three types of youngster – unhandled ones which run to the back of the stable and cower because they have had little contact with humans; well-handled ones, who are much easier; and the unruly, cocky, spoilt ones who use their own strength to try and walk all over you. The way a young horse steps out of the horsebox on arrival can tell you a lot about him; those few seconds will often be an indicator of how bold he will be.

Remember that when the young horse first arrives with you the combination of the journey and a new environment may cause him to feel shell-shocked. It is also a fact of life that if a youngster can find something to hurt itself on, unfortunately it will! I once had a youngster who got a back leg caught up in a hay manger. I wouldn't have believed this possible as it looked well out of reach, but after this incident I made a point of always feeding hay on the floor.

On the day it arrives I leave the horse to settle in quietly in its stable and get used to its new surroundings. Occasionally a young horse screams for the companion from whom it may have been parted, so it is important to have a potential replacement 'friend' in the next stable when he is left to settle. Do not turn him out in the field in case he gallops around wildly and injures himself. A large part of the horse's training at this stage is learning manners in the stable and I find that 98 per cent will settle within the hour.

TROUBLESHOOTING

What can I do to help the youngster adjust on his first day in a new place?

Generally the best policy is just to leave him quiet so he can settle in: put a little hay on the floor to pick at if he wants, and half a bucket of water. If he settles quickly, you could lead him round the yard, but use a lunge rein, and make sure the area is secure in case he 'lights up' and pulls away from you.

What do I do if the youngster is really wild?

Have a quiet horse in the next box, and just leave him to settle. If he is trying to jump out, you might have to shut his top door – though if you can secure him with a bar, or a top door with bars so he can still see out, this is better. Stand outside talking quietly to him, and do this as frequently as you can throughout the day so he gets used to your voice and smell, and hopefully gains confidence from it. As he quietens, go in and out of his box, maybe carrying water or hay, not necessarily touching him, just so he gets used to your moving around his space; it may be two or three days before you can touch him.

◄ UNLOADING: Take care when unloading him from the trailer or horsebox as sometimes youngsters won't want to wait until the ramp has been completely lowered or will want to spring off it instead of walking down it. This is why I am using a lunge line, instead of a lead rope, which will allow me to keep control while staying safe should the horse choose to leap down the ramp

➤ NEW SURROUNDINGS: Remember that this may be the first time your new youngster has seen anything other than his first home, so give him time to absorb his new surroundings and don't rush him

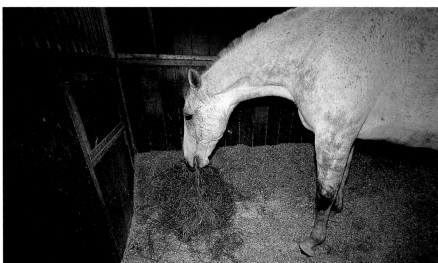

◄ SAFE FEEDING: It is important to ensure that the stable is safe, with no jutting surfaces that may cause injury. I feed all my horses their hay on the floor and I certainly would not leave a youngster with a haynet in case he got tangled up in it. If there is a built-in manger in the stable, make sure that it has no sharp edges

➤ STABLE SAFETY: Very occasionally an anxious young horse will try to jump out of the stable. If you feel this is a possibility, close the top door just for the first day. My stables have bars, which means that horses can't jump out, but they can see out, which makes life more enjoyable and interesting for them. These can be left open, or closed as the need dictates. All my stables also have windows in the rear wall which can be open or shut

Handling

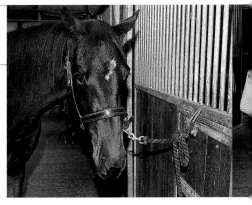

I cannot stress enough that youngsters when they come into a strange environment can be unpredictable and strong, and it is at this stage that accidents can happen. We tend to become more relaxed with familiar, older horses, but awareness is the key with youngsters; keep one eye on the front end and one on the back and be quiet in your handling. Watch his facial expression, as this will tell you if he is relaxed or frightened. In this way you will soon find out what sort of temperament he has, and if he tends to be sharp, be more wary. Generally at this stage a horse doesn't know how to be vicious – any misdemeanors will just be playfulness or nervousness.

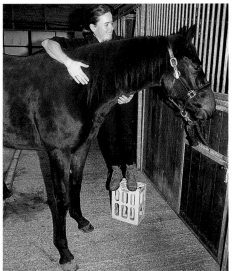

I once got sent a youngster who had obviously been running loose and had never been handled so I had to leave its headcollar on to start with, because we couldn't even catch it in the stable as it would run to the back whenever anyone came in. I ended up spending hours and hours talking quietly to him and just fiddling around with him. I would take any opportunity to give him attention so that he realised I wouldn't hurt him.

Youngsters who have been well-handled will be used to having their feet picked out and being brushed. Others may be cheeky or spoilt and pushy with big egos, and straightaway I treat them with discipline so they learn that they can't walk over me. I find it useful to carry a short length of plastic hosepipe so that if a horse tries to push past me as I come in through his door I can give him a harmless tap across the chest – unless a horse learns basic manners he will become unsafe for others to deal with. Once the horse has listened and got back, I will pat him to reward him. I certainly don't go around smacking horses with hosepipes, but, rather like carrying a whip while riding, it's a useful back-up if a horse disregards your initial request.

TROUBLESHOOTING

How can I stop my young horse pulling back when tied up?

Try using an old tail bandage instead of a piece of string to tie your lead rope to. It's stretchy and it will also snap if put under too much pressure so the horse will not injure itself. If he persists, get behind him as he pulls back, and make as if to drive him forward – clap your hands or strike a (lunge) whip on the ground behind him.

My young horse kicks when I try to pick up his back feet: what should I do?

Persevere: you must be firm but patient. Kicking is generally defensive, so just run your hand down his legs until he gets used to this – always go round all four in the same order so he knows which one you will touch next. When he accepts this, encourage him to ease the weight off the leg you are touching, always using the same voice command. Don't ask for more than an inch or so off the ground at first. However, when he knows what you want, but still kicks, tell him off sharply!

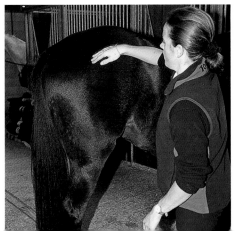

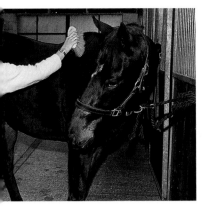

HEALTH CHECKS

Worming

Find out your young horse's worming history and treat him accordingly, though if you are in any doubt about his past management, worm him anyway. He should have been wormed about once every six to eight weeks while out in the field, and when you get him in it should be about every twelve weeks.

Feet

Ensure that his feet are trimmed, because if they are too long, this will hinder his early development; they may break or trip him up. However, it isn't necessary to put shoes on him at this stage.

Teeth

Once he is settled, think about checking his teeth. Sharp edges should be rasped, and if he has wolf teeth they may need to be removed, as they can cause pain and discomfort when there is a bit in his mouth; if the horse becomes anxious about this it will obviously hinder his training.

Feeding

Don't overdo the hard feed or he will become so strong and well that he may be too much of a handful to back successfully. I generally give a scoop of nuts and some chaff twice a day, plus hay ad lib.

◀ ◣ **TYING UP & GROOMING:** Always tie up the youngster when grooming or mucking out, ensuring that the headcollar rope is tied to a loop of string around a ring and not directly to the ring so that if he pulls back the only thing that breaks is the string. Occasionally a horse will chew the string, so the alternative is to tie the horse directly to the hook but have a little loop of string attaching the rope to the headcollar. I've never yet had a horse who wouldn't tie up, so this shouldn't be an issue

When grooming, approach quietly from the front, so the horse knows you are there, and make your way to the back end gradually. Talk to him the whole time. Take the opportunity to run your hands over his body, watching out for any sensitive areas.

Get him used to the idea of a person being higher than him, as will be the case when he is mounted or being ridden, by standing on a crate, for example. At this stage, however, I wouldn't consider doing this with a sharp or nervous youngster

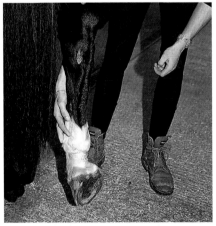

◣ **HANDLING THE FEET:** When picking up the feet, start with the front ones, then let him see that you're moving to the back end; don't make any sudden movements. If he picks up a back leg to kick, immediately tell him off with your voice, so he gets to learn different tones of voice even in the stable

Leading

The first stage in the whole backing and lungeing process is to get the horse to lead properly. Most of the youngsters, usually two-year-olds, who arrive with me have been handled, but I still like to establish a leading relationship with the horse before I do anything else with it.

Tack the horse up with a lunge cavesson and lunge rein and equip yourself with a schooling whip in the left hand, which can reach back far enough to tickle his flank if necessary, and a helper on his other side to help encourage him forward. Try not to get yourself any further forward than the horse's shoulder, and look straight ahead, encouraging him to move forward with your voice, as even at this early stage a horse can start learning to respond to the voice with instructions such as 'walk on' or 'whoa'.

➢ **LEADING:** It is important that you establish in the horse right from the start a feeling of marching forward rather than being dragged, so your body language and confidence are important. Here I am leading from the offside so that the youngster becomes accustomed to having me on the right or the left, which helps when I come to lungeing on the left and right rein.

Lungeing: getting started

The aims of lungeing are:
➤ to start training the horse to listen to and obey the rider/handler;
➤ to begin the process of getting him balanced;
➤ to teach the horse to listen to your voice commands and to obey them;
➤ to train him to go forward when asked with a flick of the lunge whip.

FIND THE RIGHT PLACE

Try to fence off the area in which you are going to lunge – this can be makeshift – as a confined area will make it easier to teach the horse what he has to do. I tend to do it in one part of the outdoor school. It's important that the footing is good, neither too hard nor too soft: deep going will hamper his movement, but equally, so will too hard a surface, like the corner of a paddock in dry, hot weather, because if a horse feels he is in danger of slipping, he will not move freely. For this reason an artificial, sand base is recommended.

When I was working with Ruth McMullen we had an ideal lunge arena where the ground was perfect which made life so much easier.

EQUIPMENT
➤ a good lunge cavesson
securely fastened so that it doesn't slip around the horse's head

➤ a lunge line attached to the central ring of the cavesson

➤ a lunge whip
to encourage the horse forward in conjunction with the voice

➤ exercise boots
to protect the horse from knocks

➤ a crash hat and gloves for the trainer and handler

ESTABLISHING CONFIDENCE: Lead the horse quietly around the area he is going to be lunged in so he realises there is nothing to worry about. If there's something there to make him spook, walk him up to it and reassure him with your voice that there is nothing to worry about. If you don't establish his confidence from the start, you will find he will cut in towards you on the lunge because he is looking at something

USING A HELPER: I generally manage to lunge a horse on my own, unless he is particularly difficult. But you should remember that this is the first time you have asked the horse to go away from you and he may try to stay close to you for security. This is when you need a helper in the initial stages to lead him quietly out onto a larger circle

HOLDING THE LUNGE REIN: It is important to keep the line neatly looped so there is no danger that the horse will become tangled if it pulls away, or that you will trip on any loops

TROUBLESHOOTING

What if I can't get my horse to lead?

Never try and drag or pull the horse (right), but get someone else to encourage him forward from the other side so he learns to go straight as well as forward.

What should I do if my horse is a handful when being led?

It is essential for safety reasons never to let the horse rush in front of you (this also applies to turning out a horse in the field). Never let his shoulder edge in front of you as this is when you could so easily be on the receiving end of the back end of a buck or a kick. You must always keep a firm hold on the lunge or lead rope and use your strength and possibly a good yank on the rope to prevent the horse getting ahead. Reward him with your voice when he settles.

Lungeing: first stage

◄ **GETTING STARTED:** It will be hard for the horse to understand at this stage that you want him to go away, as every other process so far will have involved him being close to you so he will naturally want to stay by your side. A decent length lunge whip will help to send the horse away. Point it towards his shoulder to push him out on to a bigger circle. Don't be tempted to walk towards him but try to stay in the centre of your circle so the horse goes evenly around you. You may also find it useful to get round into a more 'driving' position, a little behind the horse to push him forward

➤ **EARLY AIMS:** The time it takes to get a horse lungeing successfully will vary, but in the first session my aim will be to get him going on an even circle on both reins, just walking and trotting.
I wouldn't think about cantering at this stage, but if he broke naturally I'd allow him to canter before coming back to trot

◢ ◄ **WORKING ON BOTH REINS:** Make sure you spend an equal length of time on both reins (directions); about five to seven minutes is enough. I have often had horses who will lunge brilliantly on the left rein but won't go on the right! Even at this age, it is important to have a horse going correctly on both reins in order to rule out potential problems of one-sidedness

◄ **THE VOICE:** The voice is the key element; I find it amazing that so many people lunge in silence even with older horses at competitions

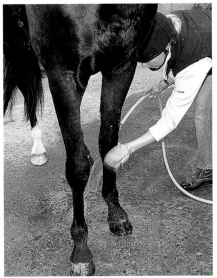

◄ **THE END OF THE SESSION:** Don't forget to reward the horse after each good session. Take him back to the yard and ask a helper to hose off his legs while you stand at his front end making him stand still. Even this activity is a lesson, in which the horse should learn to stand quietly, without fidgeting, while he has his legs hosed. If he has sweated, he needs to be quietly washed off, and again you should move quietly and slowly as this may be a new experience. Reward him with the voice when he's standing still

TROUBLESHOOTING

What should I do if my horse falls in on the lunge (see right)?

Keep a light contact on the lunge; if there's a loop the horse will keep falling in toward you, and if it's too strong a contact he will be trying to pull you out. Don't step away from *him* in an attempt to maintain the circle; he may follow you. You can't expect a youngster to trot around in a perfect circle immediately, so you will have to stay very slightly behind him so you can send him forward with your voice and by dangling the whip behind him, or towards his shoulder to stop him falling in.

What should I do about my two-year-old's sore feet?

Your youngster will be much happier and easier to train if he is comfortable, so if his feet are getting sore after a little while of working on the lunge, you should consider putting shoes on him. For his first shoeing experience it is best to have just his front feet shod in the first session. Only under exceptional circumstances would I have his back feet shod at this stage – it's simply safer without.

What should I do if my horse 'plants' himself on the lunge?

With the lunge rein not too long – a 10 to 15m circle – and keeping a light contact on the lunge rein, position yourself slightly behind him – level with his tail – and encourage him forward with your voice and by dangling the lunge whip behind him, perhaps striking the lash of it on the ground. Avoid actually flicking him with it, unless absolutely necessary.

What if I can't stop him trotting around?

Give quite sharp, intermittent tugs on the lunge rein, all the while asking the horse to 'Whoa, walk!'; making the circle

gradually smaller may encourage him to slow down. Try looking away from him, and even half turning your back on him: to the horse this is less intimidating, and the more curious will stop because they wonder where you're going. Make sure he understands your command to 'Whoa, walk!': do this when you lead him in hand, jogging along, then ask him to walk with this command so that he learns that it means 'slow down'.

After a couple of days I will think of lungeing the horse with a bridle on with the aim of teaching him how it feels to have a bit in his mouth.

I would use a rubber snaffle or a plain, lightweight snaffle – basically neither too thin nor too thick a bit, but I wouldn't bother with the noseband as he already has the cavesson, and there would be no reins.

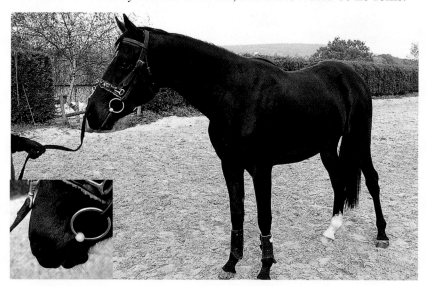

Go quietly when putting the bridle on, although it is unusual to find a horse who seriously resists, and be careful that the bit fits correctly – neither too high in the mouth, which may pinch and cause discomfort, nor too low so that it flops about, encouraging him to play around with it and get his tongue over the bit.

On perhaps day four I would introduce the roller, so that the horse gets used to having something around his middle.

After a couple of days when the horse is confident and used to these new feelings, it is time to introduce the saddle. Use an old one, if possible, and take the stirrups off it. Again, as with the roller, put the saddle on in the stable where you have more control over the horse. Get a helper to hold on to his head or tie him up while you are doing this.

⋏ ADDING A ROLLER: Always put this on in the security of the stable because then if the horse doesn't like it, he can't actually go anywhere. Be gentle as you put it on, making sure that all your movements are slow and quiet – don't just throw it on and do it up tightly. It is advisable to start with a light elastic roller before going on to a heavier, more substantial model.

Ensure that the roller is tight enough not to slip when the horse is being lunged, but not wrenched up tightly either. It is advisable to put on some sort of breastplate (see pictures) to prevent the roller slipping back – if this happens you can expect fireworks!

Remember that young horses are unpredictable and, although they don't mean to hurt you, they can knock you over very easily in fright. If the horse is tied up, make sure that you are between him and the door and not in a part of the stable where you can be trapped if he does react violently to the new restrictive sensation around his tummy.

He may try a buck when you first lunge him in the roller; if this happens make sure you send him forwards with your voice and if necessary with the lunge whip

TROUBLESHOOTING

What should I do if my horse turns away from me on the lunge?

Keep him going forwards; try attaching the lunge rein to the side ring (nearest you) on the cavesson. Work him on a smaller circle to begin with – 10 or 15m – and be sure to keep level with his shoulder: if he turns away and you are standing too far back, it will be almost impossible to bring him back on the circle. Walk round parallel with him rather than standing still in the circle centre, and encourage him forward with your voice and flicks of the lunge whip behind him; and if he threatens to turn away, give a series of short, sharp tugs on the lunge rein.

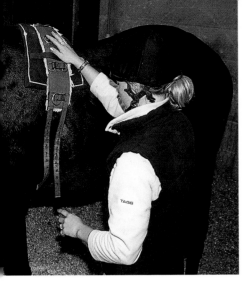

⋏ **LUNGEING IN A ROLLER:** I have added an elastic clip breastplate to ensure the roller doesn't slip back. This is the first day that this horse has worn this tack

⋖ This picture shows a youngster, Midi, happy and relaxed on the lunge, and is a good example of what can be achieved in a few days if the horse is a quick learner

INTRODUCING THE SADDLE AND SIDE-REINS

If the horse seems happy with something around him, the next stage is to put a saddle on him, which I would do in exactly the same way as the roller, in the stable. I leave the stirrups off at first and lunge with just the saddle. Very often, the youngster will react by bucking, but it is important the horse has learned to obey your voice commands and that you encourage him forward, with the lunge whip if necessary. You must send him forward through the bucking until his back comes down, he relaxes and realises he is not going to get away from the saddle. When he has happily accepted the saddle, the side-reins can be introduced. Start by attaching side-reins loosely, making sure they're slack so that the horse doesn't feel restricted. Begin with the outside rein only, very loosely, before introducing the inside one. Gradually tighten the side-reins so that there is a light contact on the horse's mouth, but not so that the head is being pulled down.

This must be a very gradual, gentle process, because if the horse becomes frightened, he could panic and rear and fall over, which will put his training back severely. Side-reins are not something I would use with a two-year-old, but they are a logical development for a three-year-old who is about to be backed.

Ready for the next step

Prepare the youngster for backing by lungeing him for a couple of days with the side-reins loosely attached to the front of the saddle (see previous page). Make the horse work up into the contact by sending him forward with your voice and a flick of the lunge whip.

Add stirrups to the saddle and get him lungeing with these swinging down so that he gets used to having something down by his side – though be aware that some horses might find the experience of something hanging by their sides quite frightening at first. However, if you have been quiet and sensible with your handling and lungeing, you should have no problems introducing your young horse to increased amounts of tack, and he should be ready to back.

➤ **LUNGEING WITH A SADDLE:** You should soon realise how happy and relaxed the horse is by his expression and way of going. This picture shows that he has accepted his new gear

PROGRESS CHECK

It's important not to move on to the next stage before your horse has successfully mastered this stage of his training. However do not delay the moment of getting a rider on. Remember that the more work a horse does, the fitter and stronger he will be. The key here is to maintain the pace of progress without creating an opportunity for a battle. Here's a checklist of watchpoints.

Is your horse happy to:
• Be tied up, groomed and have his feet picked out?
• Be led about the yard, without pulling or barging about?
• Have you standing 'above' him (for instance, on a crate), perhaps leaning over his neck/withers or back?
• Wear his tack: a light bridle, roller and breastplate, brushing boots?

Can your horse:
• Lunge on both reins without losing his balance?
• Respond when on the lunge to your vocal commands of 'Walk', 'Trot on' and 'Whoa'?

LONG-REINING

Although many trainers find long-reining has an important role to play in the breaking process, it is a real skill – not to everyone's taste and not to be attempted by a novice. I have not used it to start any of my horses and I haven't ever felt the need to use it, so I certainly wouldn't call it essential. If you decide this method *is* for you, I recommend you learn it from an expert. The following is just a brief outline of what long-reining entails.

Long-reining is the method of ground training in which two lunge lines are threaded back from the bridle through the stirrups to a person driving the horse from behind. It can be a useful way to educate the youngster about steering, forward movement and transitions before he is ridden. It can also develop strength and engagement in the back end. The down side is that if the handler is heavy handed, however unintentionally, the young horse can become frightened and panic, or develop problems with his mouth, because long-reining relies on a certain amount of pressure on the mouth.

Never try long-reining a horse for the first time in an open space; if he were to take fright and get away from you, it would be dangerous. Always do it in an enclosed space, such as a schooling arena, and with a helper to hold the horse's head and lead him to begin with. Always wear protective headgear and gloves.

Keep a safe distance from the hind legs because the horse may be frightened by the feel of lunge reins around him. Keep an eye on his ears and facial expression, as this will tell you if he is frightened or about to kick out.

Keep your aids light, the moment the horse obeys the pressure on the rein to make a downward transition, or to turn left or right, lighten your hand; if he resists, again let go.

4

Under saddle for the first time

There is no set number of days or weeks of groundwork that it should take before you can first get on a horse. Instinct will tell you when he is ready for this. I never like to rush things – but at the same time many people make the mistake of lungeing for too long so that the horse becomes too fit. It is much easier to back a horse if it is not too fit. For this reason I don't give the youngsters that have been sent to me for backing too much hard food, they will probably get half a scoop of nuts and some chaff. On the other hand trying to cut corners by riding a horse too soon will also cause problems – the horse will miss out on the crucial forming and building up of trust.

You should back your youngster in an enclosed space, and nowhere near a wire fence or road in case he escapes. I use one end of my outdoor school which is bound by a hedge on two sides and a solid fence on the short side.

It is vital that your helper on the ground should be confident and experienced, because his/her role is as important as the rider's when the horse is first backed. Now that I am a bit older – and wiser! – I prefer to be the handler these days!

Getting on

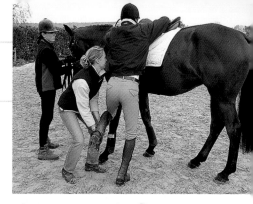

After a good lungeing session with a bridle and saddle on, quietly leg the rider up on to the horse so that they are leaning over him. Keep an eye on the horse's expression, as that will indicate to you how relaxed he is. If he is used to you leaning over him, this stage should not be a problem.

Well-fitting tack is absolutely vital at this stage if everything is to go smoothly. The saddle must not pinch, and a soft numnah can help to cushion the youngster's sensitive back. Remember that his back has never felt the pressure of a rider's weight before, and not only do his muscles have to develop, but his skin will not be used to the demands a saddle will make, which is why it is important to use a mounting block or to get a leg up. After a week or two of being mounted without care your youngster could feel sore and so will get fidgety, or try to get away from you when you want to get on. It is helpful to have a third person who can keep the horse standing still, as these pictures show. It is important he learns at this early stage that he must stand still when being mounted – a third person can concentrate solely on keeping him under control.

Make sure the stirrups are the right length and that the girth is tight enough before the rider gets on, as you don't want to be fiddling around at this stage, and a neckstrap is essential, so that if the rider loses balance they don't catch the horse in the mouth.

USING A MOUNTING BLOCK

I have a wonderfully useful mounting block in the yard and, right from the start, I make a habit of standing a youngster next to it while I stand on the block so he gets used to the idea of me being above him. If the horse is happy and relaxed, I might be tempted to lean over him.

I make a fuss of him, petting both sides of his neck and back so he gets used to a person being somewhere other than on the ground beside them. If he is looking a bit worried, I will get someone on the ground to help hold on to him and make a fuss of him, perhaps with a handful of nuts.

All this means that when we first get on the horse in the school he is already used to me leaning over him and shouldn't find it too alarming.

This two-year-old is very relaxed and from his expression is completely happy with being leaned over for the first time. This will make the task of backing him in a year's time so much easier.

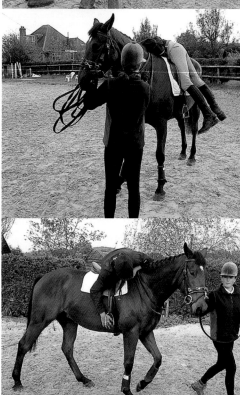

CARRYING A RIDER: Lead the horse around with the rider lying across him (in this case Steven Franks, who works for William and is quiet as a rider), just for a few steps if he is tense. Make sure that as you turn him he isn't taken by surprise by the rider, who should reassure the horse by patting him, before quietly slipping off. The handler should also keep reassuring him, while watching his expression. This is why I like to be on the ground here, as the horse will be used to my voice during lungeing. Repeat this exercise again

SITTING UP AND LEADING ROUND: Leg the rider up again so that this time he is astride the horse. To begin with he should keep his upper body fairly low on the horse's neck, getting his feet into the stirrups quickly and quietly. Lead the horse forward a few steps and if he shows no anxiety, try sitting up slowly

TROUBLESHOOTING

What if my horse freezes when he's backed for the first time?

If the lungeing process has been carried out correctly, this should not happen. However, if your horse 'plants' itself and fails to react to your voice, your assistant on the ground could help encourage the horse forward by careful use of the lunge whip in the same way as when lungeing. At the same time use your voice and legs *tactfully* to encourage him forward, but never lose your patience.

I think I'm not experienced enough to back my youngster, what should I do?

Every horse is different, with some more placid than others, but if a horse is really wild it is important to seek professional help from someone who has the knowledge and experience to sort it out – and there are many specialists in this field – because if the youngster gains the upper hand, you'll be in trouble. Never be afraid to seek help, and don't struggle on your own, because this is when accidents happen.

What do I do if the horse tries to move off when mounted?

It is important the handler makes the horse stand, but the odd step forward is preferable to the horse rearing up and fighting the restraint, in other words, don't make a major issue out of this.

Riding on the lunge

The next stage is to start lungeing the horse in the normal way. At this juncture the best way to prevent a horse misbehaving, or even thinking about doing so, is to keep him moving forward. The rider might need to sit a bit tight, but the more quickly the horse is firmly sent forward, the less likely he is to buck.

The chosen rider needs to be naturally well balanced and able to sit tight and still. Backing is not something that novice riders, who might be nervous, should undertake. However, I have had very few horses who have been difficult to back, because if all the preparation has been done carefully the horse will have built up a trust and rapport with you. Occasionally if I have felt that a horse will be tricky, I have transported him to a small indoor school so that there is no escape. Then if they really want to buck, they can't go anywhere.

Some horses react sharply to the leg and find the new sensation quite worrying, so the rider should quietly hold their leg around the horse until he gets used to it. As with horses of all ages, the important thing is to keep him moving forward with your voice and the lunge whip, so he doesn't get the chance to muck about. If the horse feels as though he might like to buck, the rider should sit behind the movement with their lower leg forward.

TROUBLESHOOTING

Should I be able to ride on the lunge on the first day of backing?

Some horses may need longer to get used to the idea that you are above them – after all, this is an entirely new experience for them. Don't ride on the lunge straight-away if you feel the horse is genuinely uncertain of this: you might need two or three days where your helper just leads you around, before progressing to lungeing. However, I find that this is not normally a problem.

What should I do if my horse runs backwards?

At this early stage the horse is almost certainly doing this because he is apprehensive, so reassure him verbally and with patting. He won't understand leg aids, so get your helper to lead him forward, just a step or two to start with. As long as he is tense and insecure, proceed gradually. Once he is more relaxed you will be able to ride him forward.

What should I do if my horse rears?

Again, almost certainly the horse is reacting like this because he feels insecure and afraid. The rider must make sure he keeps his balance to avoid pulling the horse off balance. Kicking, shouting or hitting him over the head will only add to his fear and confusion, and will probably make him more violent. As above, it is up to the handler to send him forward. This is where it is important to have an experienced handler on the ground.

◁ ⋏ **LUNGEING:** Lunge on both reins, as usual, at the walk, and if all goes well, perhaps at trot; the horse should respond to the handler's voice commands. The picture above shows that the horse is just starting to go a little too quickly. Steven is quietly holding on to the neck strap with his outside hand. It's essential for the rider to be as still as possible, relying on the handler to relax the horse

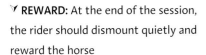

⋎ **REWARD:** At the end of the session, the rider should dismount quietly and reward the horse

⋏ **EXPECT THE UNEXPECTED:** It can be difficult for the rider to stay in balance the whole time, especially if the horse occasionally shoots forward or spooks, as he has here when he suddenly caught sight of the people at the gate. It is when the rider loses balance, which he is bound to occasionally, that the horse is even more likely to react quickly. This is why the neckstrap is important so you aren't tempted to use the rein to balance

Continuing the process

The whole backing process should be repeated next day, although I would probably cut down the amount of lungeing I did with him beforehand, and more time would be spent walking and trotting with the rider up.

I wouldn't ask the horse to canter at this stage, but if he broke into canter I would allow him to continue until he came back to trot of his own accord. Often, however, horses find it difficult to balance in canter with a rider on top.

The rider will start using the leg aid in conjunction with my voice, so that straightaway the horse is getting the idea about moving forward off the leg; he should also start taking up a light contact on the reins.

When I am one hundred per cent happy that the horse is relaxed and settled, I will let him off the lunge. By this stage the handler will have gradually become less involved, so that the horse is listening to the rider instead, to their voice and to their leg aids and accepting a light contact.

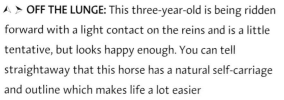 **OFF THE LUNGE:** This three-year-old is being ridden forward with a light contact on the reins and is a little tentative, but looks happy enough. You can tell straightaway that this horse has a natural self-carriage and outline which makes life a lot easier

TROUBLESHOOTING

What should I do if my horse decides to buck?

The horse won't be interested in bucking forever, so the rider should do everything he can to stay on, because once a horse has succeeded in bucking his rider off, he will almost certainly try to do it again. If the rider does come off, they must get straight back on – and if they can't, then someone else should, as soon as possible. I was once told that while trying to sit on a bucking horse if you keep your eyes on its ears and maintain the safety position behind the movement you'll stand a better chance of staying on. It's when you can't see its ears that you're in trouble. I have tried this method on a mechanical bucking bull at a party and I must say that it did help me stick on!

What should I do if the horse takes off with me?

The horse won't have the strength or the energy to keep going for too long, so stay calm, and try to bring him round in a circle. He hasn't learned any 'aids' yet, so it's no good pulling at him – he's twenty times stronger than you! Just keep bringing him round with one rein. It is important for the rider to sit very still, not letting themselves get in front of the movement, and the helper must also take control of the situation by sending the horse forward.

PROGRESS CHECK

Is your horse happy to:

• stand quietly while you get on?

• move forwards at walk and trot when you ask him, without tension or anxiety?

• slow down and halt in response to his rider's voice, and stand still whilst you get off?

Can your horse:

• walk and trot round on the lunge on both reins with a rider in the saddle without any obvious apprehension?

• respond to the voice, leg and rein aids to move forwards at walk and trot, and stay in sufficient balance to slow down and halt quietly and calmly when off the lunge?

5

Riding the three-year-old

I believe that the way a horse is ridden and managed at the age of three – or when he is broken in and first ridden – can influence the rest of his life: it is the most important stage of his career. Dealing with a three-year-old is not something that the more novice rider should attempt without help from someone more experienced, as this is when the foundation of trust, confidence and respect between the horse and his rider is established.

My overall aim when riding a three-year-old is to teach him to go forward from the leg, to respond to basic aids, and therefore, to learn manners. It is essential to manage the three-year-old so that he does not learn to get into bad habits early on. At this age a horse will be strong and unpredictable, and it is really important to be thinking one step ahead of him all the time. This will involve adopting a defensive seat in preparation for the youngster to shy or buck, and also consistently riding him forward in a continuation of his training to respond to the leg and, vitally, to be distracted out of any silly behaviour.

The first ride

Once the three-year-old is accustomed to being ridden without needing a lunge lesson first, I will get on him in the school. If he is either reluctant to go forward with you on his back or nervous, it can be dangerous to be on the hard surface of a yard. If the youngster seems to have a sensible outlook, I will get on from the mounting block. However, I always make sure I have an assistant as it is not advisable to ride a three-year-old on your own.

I will equip the horse with brushing boots to prevent knocks, but he won't have been shod behind as this could be dangerous if you fall off and get kicked. He will wear just a simple snaffle bridle, and I will also put on a neckstrap, so that if he moves suddenly and throws me out of balance, there is something to grab on to, rather than clutching a rein and hurting his mouth.

I find it safer to sit slightly behind the movement, with my lower leg forward, because I need to be ready for the very real likelihood that he will put in a buck or a spook at any moment. At this stage, I never worry about the horse's outline. The main aim is to keep him going forward with the legs while always maintaining a contact; don't let your reins go slack. Don't be tempted to niggle at the horse's head to get it into what you think is the right position. Encourage him with your voice, sit quietly and still, and keep your hands as low as possible, just above the wither, because if the horse mucks around, you will be less likely to catch him in the mouth. A horse's mouth can be wrecked at this early stage, so never fiddle with it, or pull backward on the reins.

If you do fall off, you must quietly get straight back on so that the horse quietly learns that you are not going to give up, and that he has got to behave.

➤ This sharp youngster was sent to William to bring on, and I have just climbed on him in the school. He feels pretty lively, so my hands are low and my lower leg is pushed slightly forward in a defensive position, and I am allowing him to canter forward and work off his exuberance and to settle of his own accord before I attempt any transitions. I am ready for him to misbehave, and will not unbalance him by shifting in the saddle

(inset) Having been allowed to canter and so work off some of his excess energy, the youngster is now looking more relaxed. Note that in all these pictures I am maintaining a constant contact whatever the pace, and always working the leg to the hand in order to keep a steady connection. If the rider can maintain contact with the horse, there is less likelihood of him mucking around

Each one is different

Some youngsters are completely unfazed by anything. One horse I had to ride, Midnight Magic, was so untroubled by anything that he was qualified to event at advanced level by the end of his six-year-old season (although he didn't, because that would have been too soon). He was the most straightforward horse to deal with, and seemed to get placed in competitions without trying. Sadly for me, he was sold to a Canadian rider and won his first three-day event as a seven-year-old.

By contrast, Primmore's Pride, who was bought as a foal at the same time as Midnight Magic and received exactly the same upbringing – I started them both as two-year-olds – would spook at everything he could and consequently took a lot longer to get going in competition. As a five- and six-year-old he would shy constantly while going across country – at people, at the change of terrain, at sand, flags, the lot – you couldn't go from A to B without going through the whole alphabet. But I learned to cope with it and when he turned seven he emerged as a completely different horse. His results reflected this in 2000; he was fourth, finishing on his dressage score, at his first three-day event and he won the world championship for young horses at Le Lion d'Angers in France that autumn. With Primmore's Pride, it was a case of time and patience: Rome wasn't built in a day, and he is an exceptionally intelligent horse.

TYPICAL BEHAVIOUR

I have yet to get on a three-year-old that trots immaculately around the edges of the arena at the first attempt. Most will have a good look at things, peering towards the object of suspicion and swinging their quarters out. Personally, I wouldn't consider riding a three-year-old on the road at this stage, or anywhere that wasn't a confined space (though some are not so lucky).

This is the time to establish the horse's understanding that it has to go where you want it to go. Straightaway I get the horse to listen to my inside leg, working hard to push his body towards whatever it is he's spooking at and trying to bend his head and neck away.

It is an important lesson for the horse that he realises early on that he must not rush past things; he must learn to maintain a constant rhythm, no matter what he is doing.

It is easier to control spookiness when you are going at a slower pace. Bring him back to a walk, maintain a firm contact, and if necessary let him stand and look at the object of his suspicion. Do not hassle him, and when he walks correctly past the problem in a relaxed manner, reward him, not just by patting, but with your voice, too. If you are quiet, but firm, he will eventually start to trust you in that if you say there is no problem then there isn't.

The Tourmaline Rose, the mare on whom I won the Hickstead Eventer's Grand Prix three times, is a classic example of a spooky horse – and she is tricky to this day. She looks at absolutely everything, even if there's nothing there. If I get cross, it makes it ten times worse, so I don't make an issue out of it. I ride her at whatever end of the school she's happiest in, and work her at lots of different exercises to make her listen to me, rather than leaving her with time to wonder what's behind every blade of grass.

Aside from her spooking problem, she is a brilliant, bold mare who loves competing. For an event horse, Hickstead is probably one of the most atmospheric, spooky arenas of all, but faced with the distraction of a competition, all the imaginary monsters seem to vanish

⋏ **HAVING A LOOK:** The youngster is peering at some fences piled at the side of the school and trying to swing out away from them. I have brought him back to walk and am keeping my inside leg on, bringing his body into the side of the school as well as asking him to bend his head and neck away from what he is looking at. This isn't as easy as it sounds because a newly backed three-year-old doesn't yet understand bending aids, but it is a good early lesson. In the next picture (*above right*), he is starting to come off my inside leg, but I still haven't managed to get his head and neck turned away from the cause of the spook

≺ He is starting to incline away from the inside leg and beginning to get some bend. Now he is looking much more relaxed, and I have got him to accept that the pile of fences he has been spooking at is nothing to worry about, and at the same time have been able to teach him to come round the inside leg. It is good for the horse to overcome his fear of a distraction and come out the other side having listened to the rider. Often my top horses might spook at flowers or some other distraction just before a major dressage test, and this gives me an excuse to put my leg on and say 'listen', which puts them up into another gear and can only improve their performance in the arena

➢ Make it clear that the horse knows you are pleased when he has responded correctly, and reward and encourage him throughout the schooling session so that he associates work with a happy atmosphere

The worst thing you can do if a horse really bucks and twists is to pull him up, even though that might be your natural nervous reaction. Instead, try to take up a defensive position with your lower leg forward so that your seat is more secure, keep the horse's head up and maintain a firm contact on the reins without pulling, and keep sending the horse forward out of his naughtiness. At the same time, do let the horse have a bit of a play: don't be a killjoy, and let him keep his sense of fun, because a horse with character is invariably more rewarding and successful than one without.

Any tendency to nap will probably have been caused by early signs being missed. These may only be very slight, perhaps the horse just looking towards the gateway, dropping behind your leg or hanging towards home. Even tiny signs must be immediately corrected, otherwise they can grow into a major issue. Deal with split seconds of napping by riding forward strongly. Later in the youngster's training it is common to encounter napping which is caused by the horse being unsure about the question it is being asked, such as the first time it comes to jump a ditch, or is asked to pass something on the road. Some horses are genuinely frightened, but others can just end up losing their cool and acting like a child having a temper tantrum, so that you find you are dealing with an issue that is unrelated to the initial cause of the nap. Either way you must not allow the horse to overrule you. However, if your horse does show reluctance, ask your helper to encourage him forward with the lunge whip from behind, in the same way as in the lungeing sessions. Use your voice, seat and legs to reassure and encourage the horse. Don't ignore these early tendencies to nappiness. The main reason this occurs is because the early lessons have not been thoroughly learned. You must deal firmly with napping as soon as it happens so that it does not become a real issue later on.

THE VERY SHARP HORSE

If the three-year-old is lit up when you get on him, don't pull at his mouth but allow him to canter about freely. Keep him going forward, and if he thinks about bucking, ride him forward out of it until he settles and you can slow him down without argument. Although a youngster can be very bright for the first five or ten minutes you are on his back, he will soon tire. Once he starts to relax, let him drop back to trot; ease your contact on his mouth so he can't tug you forward.

However lively a three-year-old might seem, don't be tempted to work him for more than 20–25 minutes. Don't be misled into thinking that he can do an hour's work; at this stage he isn't nearly physically strong enough. The aim is not to wear him out, but to encourage and teach him, so reward him consistently, both with your voice and by patting him, and always ride quietly with the minimum of movement.

⋏ **HIGH SPIRITS:** A typical three-year-old will often be sharp at the beginning of a schooling session. You need to ride in a defensive position until the edge of excitement has worn off. I did have one horse that had a real problem with persistent bucking, and I sent him off to someone who was very experienced with problem youngsters and had more

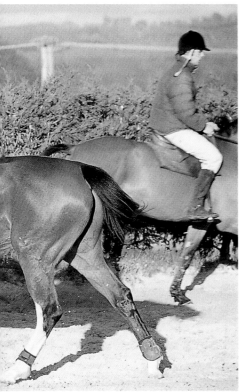

TROUBLESHOOTING

My young horse naps out to the side and won't go forward: what should I do?

As I said earlier in the chapter very often a young horse develops a napping habit because early symptoms were ignored. If I do have one that naps for any reason I will insist he goes where I want him to. For example if he is napping to the left because he doesn't want to go straight on or to the right, I will put my stick in my left hand and tap him down the shoulder in order to help me straighten him up. I might also have to use a lot more right rein – anything to get him facing in the direction I want to go – then immediately ride him very sharply forward. With a young horse it is so important to be one step ahead of him so that you can anticipate any nappiness the moment he thinks about it.

My horse rears when he doesn't want to go forward: how do I cope?

Try to anticipate when your youngster is going to rear, and prevent him from doing so by sending him strongly forward. If he does rear make sure you lean forward so that he does not lose balance and fall over backward. As soon as he comes down, use left rein and left leg behind the girth (or right rein and right leg) to bring him round, and keep turning – doing this he will find it difficult to go up again – and as soon as you can, kick him forward. (Note these aids are only to prevent him rearing.)

My horse plants himself and refuses to budge: how do I make him move?

You might need someone on the ground to help you send him forward with a lunge whip; try and sort this out at home, before you get stuck when hacking out. Carry a long schooling whip, and try and drive him forward with frequent taps on his stifle and hocks and the top of his quarters. If he still won't budge, try moving him with left rein and left leg behind the girth (or right rein and right leg), and if he takes even just a step or two, then try sending him forward. The lesson of going forward from the leg must be firmly instilled right from the start.

If my young horse doesn't want to go, he stops and then runs backward: should I hit him?

Again, find any reasonable way to make the horse go forward from your leg: make a rule, too, of always riding him firmly forward up to a constant contact; carry a schooling whip, and never just slop along on a loose rein – then he will always take advantage of you! Work on always keeping his attention: bend him this way and that, and do lots of transitions. Anticipate when he might be awkward, and try and keep his head and body bent away from the potential hazard. To stop him running back, try turning him/bringing him round, as already discussed, and kick him forward as soon as you can!

TIP Any of these problems might be the horse's way of telling you that something hurts, particularly in a young horse in these early days of riding him: maybe his saddle is pinching, or he has a sore tooth, or his girth area or mouth is tender, or his hooves are wearing down too much and his feet are sore. Check all these things before you get over-insistent about him going forward.

suitable facilities for dealing with it, in this case the restricted area of an indoor school. All horses are different, and although most are inherently obedient and willing to please, you will get the occasional difficult one, and with these you must seek expert help before the problem escalates. Never get into a battle you aren't capable of winning

Establishing the basics

Once the three-year-old has settled while being ridden around the arena, I will start to do some basic transition (change of pace) work. Repeated transitions will help the horse learn the different aids. I take my time over downward transitions because it is important that the horse is not resisting or fighting but accepts the hand as a slowing aid. Avoid the temptation to pull, take your time, and use the closing on of your leg instead and continual vocal aids. Always ride quietly, and do not expect a three-year-old to be able to do transitions like an older horse.

WALK TO TROT

Use your legs and voice, and allow the horse to trot on, whilst maintaining a constant rein contact. Remember that the main aim at this stage is to teach the young horse to respond to a light aid, so if he seems lazy or dead to the leg, don't keep flapping them! If there is no response, give him one good sharp kick and tickle him with the whip. At this stage the less forward-thinking horse will get into the habit of being dead to the leg if you endlessly 'nag' him.

TROT TO CANTER

You cannot expect a three-year-old to perform the perfect strike-off into canter. Most of them tend to run into canter, but I would sooner allow them to run for a few strides than pull them around and kick. Stay still in the saddle, ask with the leg, and maintain an even rein contact. Don't tip your body forward and get ahead of the movement – a common rider error – or you will unbalance him. The young horse will tend to fall into canter, rather than push from behind, so do not expect him to be able to hold himself in balance in canter. Most youngsters will scoot about a bit, find it difficult to maintain balance, and fall back into trot. Ride forward, and if he does fall back into trot, allow him to re-establish himself at that pace before asking him to canter again. It is only a matter of time before a youngster will find a better strength and manage to hold himself together in canter.

USE YOUR VOICE

➤ The voice aid is extremely important, especially at this early stage of training. Not only will the horse be reassured and encouraged, but also this will help him relate to the lessons he learned on the lunge, where the voice aid was predominant.

⩘ **WORKING ON TRANSITIONS:** As this is a fairly sharp horse (you can see that his attention is rather anxiously focused back at me while I'm riding), it is important to keep a secure leg. I have also got a slightly forward seat and upper body position because, as he is sensitive, I don't want to lose my balance backward. If I do, he is the type to shoot forward. When teaching transitions, your bodyweight and balance give the horse as many signals as your hands. Here (*top left*) I am lightening the reins without losing contact and keeping the horse moving forward up to the bit.

Young horses tend to run into canter (*top centre*) but I am not pulling him back and restricting the forward movement. It is also typical for the unbalanced youngster to fall back into trot (*top right*), and you will need to allow him to settle before asking for canter again.

At the second attempt (*left and above*) the youngster made a much more assured transition into canter

CANTER TO TROT

Once you have got going, don't be tempted to canter endlessly round and round; try to put in a trot transition before the horse breaks into trot of his own accord, when you sense he is about to lose the canter – you'll find that his stride will get longer and flatter when he is about to break. To make the transition, stay sitting up, and don't let the horse drag you forward when he falls back into trot. Think 'trot' to yourself, and lighten your contact as he does the transition to prevent you from restricting the forward movement. Don't tip forward, or the horse will fall on to its forehand and fall behind the leg. For the rider, the downward transition is almost more of a mental than physical process. Sit still, hold with your body, and mentally stop cantering while keeping the horse going in front of your leg.

TROT TO WALK

Remember that transitions are supposed to be progressive and smooth, not jolting and abrupt. I would rather allow the horse to take a relatively long time making the transition to walk, because it is especially in this transition that you see horses flopping on to their forehand, shortening their stride, and unable to establish a good walk. Gradually slow the trot rhythm by rising a little slower, staying tall in your body, closing your leg around the horse, and holding with your upper body and arm. Ask the horse verbally to walk, and you will feel him starting to come back into walk. Again, it is essential you don't pull him back with your hand, but allow him to walk forward.

WALK TO HALT

As before, stay quiet, close your leg, and ask the horse to halt with your voice. If he won't, ride him up to a nearby fence or hedge, keeping him straight between your hands and legs and asking him to halt at the fence. When he does, it is important to reward him, both verbally and by patting. At this stage there is no need to worry about his head position; just allow him to stand and relax.

➤ Even at this young age, I try to get the horse turning correctly. Many of us may have been taught as children to 'turn with your hands' but this is, in fact, not the right way to go about it. You must ask a horse to turn by using your legs, seat and body. It is tempting to pull too much on one rein without using sufficient leg on the opposite side; this just results in the horse's head being pulled round without the rest of the body bending after it. Instead, apply your inside leg, ask the horse to turn through your arm and apply the outside leg to get the horse to come round, staying upright in your body with your shoulders parallel to the horse's shoulders. It helps to have your stick in the outside hand to rub down the horse's shoulder as you ask him to turn.

⋏ **DOWNWARD TRANSITIONS:** When changing pace from trot to walk (*top left*), it sometimes helps the young horse to ride with a light seat or slightly off his back when you first start to canter. Try and keep the transition progressive by slowing your rising, which slows the rhythm and keeps your leg on so he stays forward

TROUBLESHOOTING

My youngster won't stand still in the halt.

If the horse is a fidgeter, don't make an issue of it but ask a helper to give him a piece of grass or a mint to concentrate on. This is all part of the process of establishing a well-mannered horse; with time and patience he will learn to stand quietly. Again, always reward good behaviour, be consistent, and keep your cool if things don't go according to plan.

My horse yaws horribly when I try to turn him. What should I do?

You are probably using too much hand and not enough leg. The idea is for the horse to be bending around the inside leg with the outside leg asking him to come around – don't pull him around with your hand. Try using a neckstrap. If you hold on to it with your inside hand, that will stop you moving the hand too much.

When can I ride out?

When I am one hundred per cent happy that the horse has a proper understanding of what is being asked of him, I will take him out for a hack, always in company. If the horse has learned the basic aids successfully, you should not encounter any problems. I have invariably found that the youngster behaves well.

Never go out hacking on your own with a three-year-old, because if you get into difficulties it will be very hard to deal with them alone, and you want to avoid a confrontation at this stage. Always be quiet but firm, so the horse realises he has to pass suspicious-looking objects – press with the opposite leg to the object and turn his head away slightly – and that he has to go where you tell him. I cannot stress enough that you must avoid a battle you aren't capable of winning.

6

Early flatwork training

Most of the four-year-olds I am sent to ride arrive in the autumn, at the end of the competition season, unless they have particular promise for Burghley Young Event Horse classes, in which case they will have arrived earlier. Therefore, a four-year-old will have been turned out for anything from four to eight months since being broken. When it arrives back in my yard I always err on the side of caution: so, rather than get straight on its back, I will lunge it with tack on to settle it and get its back down.

At this stage it is important to give the youngster time to mature and gain strength. It is too much to expect a three-year-old to work right through into its four-year-old year without a break, not only from the point of view of physical strength, but also in mental stability and self-assurance – and even four-year-olds are not physically mature enough to be worked hard. It is, however, surprising how much they remember from when they were backed and first ridden.

My main aim is to progress quietly with short but frequent sessions in order to strengthen the young horse physically and build communication. His work must be varied so he keeps a bright outlook on life. I make constant changes of direction, circling (often in a spiralling effect), looping and lots of transitions to help him engage his back end. I constantly give him things to think about, so without realising it he will be learning the different leg aids and focusing more and more on the rider.

Rider position

As with the three-year-old, your principal aims are still to have the horse going forward, straight and in front of your leg, but now you can ask him to form a rounder, more controlled outline. This must be done with the seat and legs. I find when teaching that a common fault is for riders to use their hands too strongly in an effort to pull the horse's head into an outline. If done like that, the outline will be false: it will look stiff and forced, and the stride will be short and restricted because tension will be compromising the power of his movement. When an outline is achieved in the correct way, the horse feels light, he will look loose and supple, and will be in self-carriage.

Be consistent with your contact, even if the horse tries to resist it by dropping behind it or by sticking his head in the air. He needs to learn that he can't get away from your hand, but also that he can trust you to be consistent.

A true rounded outline only comes from the connection of the horse's back end into the hand. Many young horses (and older ones who have been incorrectly schooled) try hard to avoid rein contact. I like to think of the rider's arm being an extension of the rein, with a straight line from the bit to the elbow; the rein should be still yet elastic in tension, and never loose or in loops. The arm must be supple and not locked, as maintaining the light contact on the mouth comes mostly from the rider's elbow, and the sponging of the fingers in conjunction with the leg which pushes the horse forward into the contact. The main aim is to achieve a responsive horse that moves in self-carriage, without leaning on the rider.

It is very easy to tip your body position too far forward when riding green horses. They inevitably go on their forehand and can pull you forwards with them.

THE HORSE'S MOUTH IN YOUR HANDS

In these early days the horse's mouth can be easily ruined. It amazes me how some riders don't seem to realise how sensitive the horse's mouth is, for there is a difference between holding the horse to slow it, and pulling it. If the hand is used roughly and inconsistently and is constantly niggling at the bit, then the horse's mouth will become dead and unresponsive.

The rider must be aware of carrying their own hands and making sure that their reins are not too long to maintain a useful contact – a surprisingly common fault. Never pull back on the horse, whether for a downward transition or when trying to achieve more engagement. Keep your hands still, and hold the horse with your seat and back. If the hand has to pull backward in order to maintain contact, it means the rider has not used sufficient back, seat and leg, and the horse will either lean and dive onto its forehand, or it will shorten its neck.

◀ **RIDER POSITION:** (*top*) The correct rider position, sitting straight in the saddle, with a secure, effective position, the heel down in the stirrup, the leg on the girth and a light rein contact (*centre*) The wrong position! The lower leg is too far back and the rider is perched on the front of the saddle which will result in them rocking forward and their hands becoming fixed (*bottom*) Wrong again! An old-fashioned, back-of-the-saddle hunting position which will encourage the horse to hollow away from the rider's seat. Having said that, it can also be a useful safety position on a bucking horse – but only then

◥ **RIDER POSITION:** (*top left*) The stirrups are too short and the hands are too low. As a result, I am pulling the horse's head down, and with the lower leg too far back and therefore ineffective, the horse has fallen on its forehand with its hocks strung out behind it

(*top right*) Wrong again! If the stirrups are too long, the rider will have difficulty pressing the weight into the heels, which will cause them to lose their balance and rely on their hands for balance

(*bottom left*) Another wrong position. The reins are too long and my hands are too far back – they are not carried independently, and are ineffectual

(*bottom right*) Right! The correct length of stirrup and the desired straight line from the elbow down the rein to the bit. Here, my hands are neither too low, pulling down, nor too high, holding the horse up. The horse is slightly behind the vertical, and his poll, which needs to be the highest point, is too low – but a five-year-old is not going to show the perfect outline at this stage of his training

Straightness

Ruth McMullen instilled in me the belief that any problems that occurred could usually be traced back to the rider's position and lack of straightness. As a result, I am now conscious of trying to sit straight and in total balance.

Some horses are more sensitive than others, but I've never yet found one that will go straight with a crooked rider aboard. So often when I am watching dressage I see riders losing marks because their own crookedness is making the horse crooked. If you aren't sure about your own straightness, ask someone to watch you from behind to check that your weight isn't falling more heavily on one side.

The rider can maintain straightness by not letting their inside hip collapse but by remaining tall in the saddle, by keeping the inside leg long and pressed down and by mentally dropping the outside shoulder. It can help to look behind you, over the outside shoulder, as an exercise, or if the horse is sensible enough, put both reins into the outside hand and put your inside hand behind your back and place it on your outside shoulder blade.

Exaggerated this may be, but crookedness really is a common fault

EXERCISES FOR STRAIGHTNESS

➤ Ride without stirrups and take your thighs away from the saddle. As soon as you can do this exercise at the trot and canter without slipping, you'll know that you're sitting straight. It's quite hard work – and you musn't rely on your hands for balance – but it will soon show you whether you are slipping one way or the other as you will find yourself gripping particularly hard with one thigh. The combination of this and the inevitable pull on the rein to keep you in balance will result in the horse losing straightness. He will be receiving a mixed message: the inside rein is asking him to bend but your position is making it difficult for him to do so. This is how horses become stiff and one-sided. Often during lessons pupils will ask me why their horse is so unresponsive on one side of its mouth; it is nearly always due to the rider not sitting straight.

➤ Another useful exercise in instilling straightness of position is to ride with both hands touching. In doing this, if corrections need to be made to the way the horse is going, you will have to do it with your leg and seat while maintaining the horse's forward momentum. Remember, though, that 'forward' doesn't equal 'faster': it simply means that the momentum is coming from the back end through to your contact.

⋏ **STRAIGHTNESS:** A very straight horse, as desired – in fact everything is straight and even – apart from my hat, which seems to be sitting on one side of my head!

⅄ WORKING DOWN THE CENTRE LINE: When changing direction, make sure the horse is going forward and straight in front of your leg. Your inside leg should be quietly asking for a little bit of bend through the horse's body and ribs, while the outside leg will bring the horse round into the new direction.

A common fault is that riders turn the horse with too much inside rein and not enough outside leg, so that the horse falls out through the shoulder. If this isn't corrected with the outside leg, the horse will get stiffer and heavier on the inside rein. Conversely, when a horse falls in through its turns, it is probably due to lack of inside leg pressure. Keep the horse's head and neck straight, and then you will be aware of what is going on underneath you.

Here I am working the horse on a turn down the centre line, concentrating on straightness; as you can see (*above left*), the horse is slightly tilting his head. This is not an indication of a problem with his mouth – people often think a horse is tipping his head because of a problem in the mouth – it is because he is slightly falling out through his right shoulder. This would result in him being crooked down the centre line. Contrast this with the final two views (*top centre and top right*), where in a good turn his head and neck are straighter, and he is much straighter when he comes on to the centre line.

⅄ ESTABLISHING STRAIGHTNESS: This exercise, with a stick threaded through both elbows behind my back, helps to establish rider straightness and get my shoulders back. Even more importantly, it teaches the rider to use the seat and back as an aid – in fact these are the most crucial aids of all. Note, however, that I am performing this exercise while riding an experienced and steady horse, Supreme Rock (Rocky). This is not an exercise to be tried on a young or difficult horse, but on a reliable one that you know well.

⅄ CARRYING YOUR HANDS: A useful exercise, with the stick held under the thumbs, to ensure that the rider is carrying their hands, rather than leaning on them, and that the hands are level.

The paces: walk and trot

THE WALK

You may not be able to work on this pace at the start of a session, as the horse may be too fresh, but time does need to be spent on the walk because if you don't get it right, more than likely the other paces won't come right, either.

Try to keep the same walk, whether you are riding on a long or a short rein. Many riders don't think about this enough, and allow the horse to anticipate as soon as they pick up the reins. This can create a boring habit and often the restless, jogging, short-striding horse is like that because the rider has not worked hard enough at maintaining a consistent walk.

The horse must learn to stay relaxed and in a consistent, regular stride even if you have picked up the reins; if he thinks he can rush and dictate the pace, his stride will become shorter and shorter. I try to get the stride as long as possible by allowing him to stretch and have the time to lengthen.

THE TROT

My main aim is to get the horse moving forward in its own natural rhythm. Some horses naturally have a wonderful metronome-like beat; others don't, and it is important to train these to maintain a consistent rhythm. If the horse finds it difficult to keep a rhythm, establish a steady beat in your own head and keep him moving forward to it; a steady, regular pace will give the horse time to move and to cover more ground. Sometimes people think that if the horse has a short, shuffling trot, the answer is to hurry it out of it. This is actually one of the most usual ways that a young horse begins to lose rhythm and balance, especially around turns and corners.

Don't expect a four-year-old to balance himself when ridden deep into corners because he hasn't learned to take the weight on his back end, and isn't physically mature and collected enough. Instead, work him in shallow loops and serpentines that he will be able to manage, so his balance is being tested sufficiently without asking too much of him.

RESISTANCE: If the horse resists, as it is here (*left*), it is important still to maintain the consistent contact and keep the hand quiet; don't be tempted to try and pull the horse back down. Keep your leg on and your hand still and eventually the horse will realise it is only fighting itself and will find that it is much more comfortable to work into the contact rather than to resist it (*centre*). The horse won't accept the contact if you take the short cut by niggling him or by pulling his head down

(*right*) Here, because I am sitting behind the movement, pulling on the rein this is causing the horse to resist. Note that this problem is being caused by the rider, as opposed to the horse actually resisting. Be aware of what you are doing as a rider: self-awareness is half the art of producing a young horse, evaluating if it is *you* that are causing the problems

ESTABLISH THE WALK: A relaxed, yet purposeful medium walk. It is important to establish a willing, rhythmic, consistent walk from the start, as horses can get into bad habits of jogging or poking along.

A 'happy', relaxed free walk

BEHIND THE VERTICAL: The five-year-old Best of All (Muffin) is a horse whose natural inclination is to shorten his neck and drop his head behind the vertical. This is more difficult to correct than being above the bit. The rider should work on allowing the rein contact to be taken forward through the arms, which should have the leverage, not the hands. In the photo on the right I am pushing down the rein and, even though Muffin's head is still slightly behind the vertical, his way of going is much softer; you can see the difference in my arms in the two pictures. This position allows the horse to stretch down and take the rein, rather than having it thrown at him, so the contact is still there

A GOOD TROT: A steady, rhythmic trot. The horse is carrying himself well and really using his shoulder

A MATURE TROT: This what we're aiming for – the advanced horse, Rocky, performing medium trot. He is really working through and has the established outline one would hope for in a horse of his age and experience. To be critical, his mouth is open a little

The paces: canter

At first, a young horse will be unable to hold the canter for too long. However, although you can't expect him to perform a collected canter, you can aim to have him carrying himself – though sometimes you will have to let him go faster than you might like so he can achieve that.

When I feel that the horse is ready to be asked to hold a slightly shorter canter, I would take up a 20m circle in trot, then establish a good, forward working canter. Then, by sitting very tall so that I'm holding the horse with my seat, back and hand, I would try and 'concertina' him together, softening my hand so that he is not leaning on me. I would only keep him like this for about half a circle, before either bringing him back into trot or allowing him to go forward into a faster canter. Try to ask him for the transition to trot, rather than just allowing him to break. By doing this exercise regularly, you will find that the horse can hold a shorter canter for longer each time.

⋏ **TRANSITION TO CANTER:** A smoother transition, but I have tipped forward slightly so the first stride the horse takes *(right)* will be very much on his forehand

➤ ⅄ I am sitting up and staying still. By repeating transitions, the horse accepts the lighter aid and stays in balance, and so straightaway the canter is where I want it

The incorrect strike-off can be caused when the weight of the rider is thrown onto the horse's outside shoulder; this often happens when the rider leans (incorrectly) to the inside when asking for canter. If a horse is consistently striking off on the wrong leg, first check whether your position is the cause. Lack of balance in either you or your horse will certainly be the root of the problem.

A terrible transition! I have asked with too much body and hand and the horse is resisting. I am also leaning in. You can see by the horse's expression that he is not amused!

It is common for young horses to be on the forehand because they are immature and haven't got the strength to take their weight on their hocks. Young horses also grow in stages, the back end growing up a bit, then the front; often you will see a young horse with a higher back end. It is usually between the ages of four and six that their front end finally matures and their shoulder and wither develop and become more level with the back end.

This physical state doesn't mean, however, that the four-year-old should be allowed to learn to lean. Stay tall in the saddle so that you can't be tipped forward and gently tweak with your fingers, at the same time giving a little double nudge with the leg, to get the head up before softening your hands. Never hold his head up in a constant pull, or the horse will simply lean on you, and you will feel as though you are holding up a ton of weight.

TROUBLESHOOTING

My horse doesn't seem to concentrate on his work. What am I doing wrong?

Any horse, and particularly an intelligent one, will quickly get bored by trotting round in endless circles, so vary what you do: lots of transitions, introduce leg-yielding, use groundpoles to keep his interest and challenge him a bit. Perhaps your schooling sessions are too long – twenty minutes is plenty for a youngster; he won't concentrate if he is tired.

How can I stop my horse being lazy in schoolwork?

If he is truly lazy you will need a schooling whip and spurs to encourage him to be sharper: constant kicking will very quickly make a horse completely dead to the aids. First you squeeze, then you kick once, then you tap with the whip: it is imperative that the horse learns to react straightaway to your aid. Try schooling while hacking out: you can do most schooling work – transitions, leg-yielding – anywhere: in a lane, over a field, through a wood. Remember that a real youngster may not be truly lazy, but just unco-ordinated, physically immature and rather naïve.

How can I stop my horse throwing his head around?

Either he just hasn't learned to accept the contact, or something hurts. First check his mouth and teeth; check that his tack isn't pinching (saddle too narrow/wide, bit too high/low); have his back checked: if he is in pain when he works he will never settle. If you are pretty sure nothing is hurting him, then keep your hands as still as you can, and do your best to maintain a steady, even, light-to-firm contact on the reins, even if he chucks his head in the air; you will need to keep him going forward with a steady leg pressure, too. If he shows any sign of relaxing and dropping his head sensibly, ease with your fingers, thereby lightening the contact a little – this is his reward.

My horse falls in on turns and circles: what can I do?

Keep him in balance by using more inside leg on the girth, supported by steady contact on the outside rein, and outside leg behind the girth. Make sure you are sitting straight, and not collapsing the inside hip: although your upper body may be inclined to the inside of the circle, your bodyweight may be on the outside seatbone, and this will compromise your inside leg aids. You may need to lift your seat and actually move your weight across the saddle and more on to the inside seatbone; then make your inside leg long so your lower leg can come into firm contact with the horse's side.

Progress on the flat

At five, when the young horse is more upright, balanced and forward-moving, I would start quietly introducing some more demanding and suppling movements, and I would ask for more accuracy. I would want the horse to be working at home at a higher level than the standard he will have to perform at during his first competition, just as I would expect him to be able to jump a decent-sized course of show jumps before taking him cross-country schooling. On the flat, for instance, I would like the horse to be balanced while doing 10m (33ft) and 15m (49ft) circles at trot, although the British Eventing novice test only demands a 20m (66ft) circle.

When preparing for a first dressage test, at whatever level, I would ride through it several times, so that the movements flow and you are thinking about setting the horse up for the next required movement even before you have finished the one before. At this stage, I also set myself and the horse high standards of accuracy. I pick a point in the school where I will require the horse to perform a transition, and I work to prepare him sufficiently so that it does happen at that marker. I also work a lot at home on the size of circles, so that a 15m circle really *is* 15m and not a little too big or slightly too small. This not only teaches the horse that he must go exactly where you want him to go, but it will also teach the rider discipline, with the result that you will naturally perform more accurately in competition and not lose marks.

Suppleness and obedience on the flat is, however, not just for competition; it will make the horse a much more pleasant ride and a safer hack if you have control and can make it go where and at what pace you want. The aim is to have the horse carrying himself and for the rider to be doing as little as possible.

Sometimes riders overwork their horse at a movement they find difficult, and the horse loses heart; he associates flatwork with doing something he finds hard. Therefore, it is just as important to work a horse on movements he finds easy; a contented, confident horse who enjoys his work will be much more useful to you. If you work too hard on his weaknesses, he may become either tense and wound up, or quite the opposite, lazy and behind the leg, and will certainly lose heart.

KEEP IT INTERESTING: Maintain the horse's interest and balance by using frequent changes of direction and bends on both reins. Here the horse is upright and balanced as we weave around markers in the school but it looks as though I am holding him up. He is a little overbent and needs to learn more self-carriage

My horse runs into canter, and feels long and unbalanced when he comes back to trot.

Establish a steady, regular trot, ride a 20m circle, and then ask him to canter; if he still runs, try spiralling into a smaller circle at trot, then go to canter. Do frequent trot to canter/canter to trot transitions, to shorten him. This should help him stay balanced as he goes into trot – and make sure you keep the leg on, because even if he runs, if you forget the leg pressure and rely on your hands only, he will hollow and be even harder to correct. If he still feels long, try canter to trot, then quickly to walk transitions, so he is thinking 'slower' all the time.

My horse won't strike off on the left/right lead in canter

Most horses favour one lead rather than the other, and it is generally practice and habit that will solve this problem. To begin with, make sure you are sitting straight and square: you will only make it harder for the horse if you are crooked. Try leg-yielding (see page 80) into a corner, then asking for canter as you turn through it: leg-yielding gets the hindleg stepping under the quarters, and so in a good position for a correct strike-off. Make sure *your* outside leg is behind the girth, so he can't swing his quarters to the outside of the circle. Some people put a groundpole in the corner to help teach the horse this.

Lateral work

When the horse is five years old it is enough to teach him basic lateral work. I would not introduce movements such as half-pass and pirouette until he is six or seven. However, it is important to teach horses to come away from the leg because these exercises will improve their suppleness; it also helps to correct any straightness problems. For example, if a horse falls out from the shoulder I will work on this by riding shoulder-in, which will exaggerate the correction.

It is important not to make an issue of lateral work at first. Some horses are stiffer laterally than others and can tighten up. With these horses I only do a small amount of lateral work, and then move on to something else.

LEG-YIELDING

The idea of leg-yielding, a suppling exercise, is to make the horse step away from the rider's leg into the opposite rein, moving both forward and sideways, whilst bending around the leg he is stepping away from, without losing straightness. As with any new exercise, it must be done quietly and sympathetically, as the horse may not at first fully understand what you are asking. Only ask for a few steps at a time, at the walk, and ride him forward immediately after. To move him away from your left leg, apply the left leg a handspan behind the girth, keep the right leg just behind the girth as support and ride him forward. The left hand should maintain a light contact, so that the head is flexed slightly left, and the right hand maintains balance and freedom. When the horse is happy leg-yielding in both directions at walk, practise it at the trot.

SHOULDER-IN

This is another useful suppling exercise which helps to lighten the forehand, engage the hindquarters and straighten the horse. It is a three-track movement, with the inside foreleg on one track, the inside hind leg stepping into the same track as the outside foreleg and the outside hind leg

Movements such as shoulder-in can make the horse more controllable if he has a tendency to shy, as his head is bent away from the frightening object.

on a third track. Again, the emphasis must be on the horse's straightness, as without that you cannot expect a horse to do a correct shoulder-in. Many people make the mistake of either too much or too little bend; the hindlegs should stay straight with the shoulder coming across.

Do this in walk at first, preparing the horse around a corner on a 10m circle so that he has every chance of getting the movement right. The inside leg pushes him round and the outside rein brings the shoulder in, while the inside rein causes a slight inside bend and the outside leg stops the quarters from swinging outwards. Keep riding forward to prevent wiggling.

⋏ SHOULDER-IN: *(left)* A clear example of far too much bend in the shoulder-in. The shoulder is out and no angle is being shown. My inside hand has gone too far across Matter of Fact's (Matty's) neck, creating too much neck bend

(right) A better angle has been achieved because I have thought more about it before the corner. To be critical, Matty could have a touch more bend, but this is still good positioning for a five-year-old who is just learning

⋎ A good example of shoulder-in. Rocky is in a good position and I am looking up into my imaginary mirror, to keep me straight. The horse, however, is looking at the photographer!

Too much pressure on the outside rein will restrict the horse so that it won't have sufficient bend; the role of the outside rein should be supportive, as opposed to restrictive.

A common problem in shoulder-in is when the rider collapses their inside hip as they apply the inside leg; the horse is then thrown off balance and is more likely to fall out through the shoulder, because he can't bring it across. Be aware of keeping the inside leg long, and of keeping the horse in front of you. I try to imagine a mirror at one end of the school; I look straight at it to remind myself to sit upright all the time.

REIN-BACK

This movement should not be taught too early, but is another exercise that is useful when hacking out, for example when opening gates or moving out of the way, and it will lighten the forehand.

Before attempting the rein-back, ask for a square halt. It is more important with a young horse to have the correct transition into the halt, rather than fiddling with it, but when the horse is more established you must work towards getting him to stand square. A horse which has correct conformation – a leg in each corner – and is balanced will naturally halt square, but if he has left a leg sticking out, the rider should be able to feel this and nudge him into a more square position.

Thus, if he has left a back leg, nudge it up with your leg on that side (ie if he has left his right hind, take your right leg back and nudge it up). At the same time, hold the horse with your hands so that he doesn't think he is being asked to go forward. If he has left a front leg back, ask the youngster to step up to this leg by pushing your own leg further forward behind the shoulder. You will know from the horse's reaction whether you have got enough pressure in the contact.

When you want him to rein back, it can be useful to have a helper on the ground to push the horse gently backward as you apply the aids. It is quite common for a young horse to resist the rein-back because he doesn't understand what you are asking. Some horses also find it difficult to take the weight on their hocks at this stage. If you feel the horse is threatening to go up on his hind legs, get the helper to do the pushing back and use your voice to ask the horse. Repeat this exercise a few times until he feels happy about it, and then try to do it without your helper.

If the horse runs back too quickly, it probably means that you are applying too much hand, so walk him forward again. The horse should be taking each step backwards in conjunction with you; you should be working together.

ᴀ **REIN-BACK:** At a square halt I lighten my seat before I ask for the rein-back. If you sit too deep and heavy, the horse will hollow underneath you and find it difficult.

Quietly take your lower leg further back. Ask with a bit of give in the left rein and right leg and then with the opposite rein and leg. Don't pull or saw, but allow the back end to come up underneath you. Only expect one or two strides backward, and then walk the horse forward

Introducing jumping

The aim when introducing the young horse to jumping is for it to be simply a continuation of flatwork training – but with fences in the way. Again, the idea is to interfere as little as possible with the horse and have it working so it is cantering around between fences in self-carriage. The *rider's* job is to present the horse at a fence in a balanced way, while the *horse's* job is to jump the fence.

I am always tempted to pop the three-year-old over a little fence, whether on the lunge or ridden, because I'm dying to know what sort of feel it gives me when it leaves the ground. However, I would not start jumping a horse that young because, with a few exceptions, he is generally not strong enough or sufficiently balanced in the canter to be able to jump well with a rider on top.

Do not, therefore, be dismayed if your four-year-old feels completely at sea and uncoordinated over his first few fences. When we bought Teddy Twilight as a four-year-old he jumped well loose, but when first ridden to a fence he seemed to have no respect for it and felt as if he had no scope. I seriously thought that we had made a big mistake in buying him, but I then realised that he just wasn't physically mature enough, and so we gave him some more time. As a five-year-old he was a completely different horse and he now has a very impressive and careful jump.

Rider position and the canter

A common fault when jumping is for riders to become obsessed with the horse's striding as he comes into a fence, and with the correct point of take-off. However, worrying about meeting the fence wrong will result in the rider interfering with the horse, either checking him too much in front of a fence, or moving him forward too strongly or too fast so he is out of balance and losing the strength from his back end.

What people forget is that a horse can only be a maximum of half a stride wrong – not a very big distance – and if he can't cope with that it is usually the result of the rider interfering so that either the horse has lost impulsion and doesn't have the energy to get himself out of trouble or has been hassled out of his rhythm and has become too long and flat to be able to push over the jump. A horse that accelerates too much in the last few strides has usually been ridden by someone who habitually 'fires' him at the fence at the last minute, thinking (wrongly) that this is the way to engender enough impulsion.

With his showjumping background, my husband William has helped me more than anyone to realise the importance of the horse carrying itself in canter with enough 'engine'. The horse should do this without you feeling you've got to hold them together or ride with too much leg. The leg must, of course, be close, but it should be a light leg with the pressure coming on the stride of take-off.

The most important thing for the rider to work on is the quality of the horse's canter and rhythm, then he has every chance of meeting the fence in balance and correctly and, thus, jumping it correctly also.

It is important that the rider's stirrups are not too long so that he/she can keep their balance. Long stirrups lead to the rider bouncing out of balance in the saddle and pulling on the horse's mouth; too short, and the rider will get in front of the movement, something to be avoided at all times, especially with youngsters. Not only will the horse be thrown on to his forehand, but the rider's seat will be less effective and secure, and if the horse stops or hits the fence, they are more likely to fall off.

If the rider's leg is secure – and this is made easier if the heel is firmly down – the upper body is more likely to be in the correct position. Often when I'm teaching, I see riders thrusting their upper body forward as they land, even over a small fence, but this is in fact unbalancing for the horse: the rider should just try and concentrate on keeping their balance. This applies equally to the approach, the jump over the fence and the landing on the other side.

Be ready to allow the horse freedom of its head. This doesn't mean throw the reins at it, but a young horse can put in some big, awkward jumps, and if you can keep your lower leg forward and slip the reins through your fingers, you will avoid catching him in the mouth.

Poles/crosspoles

POLES ON THE GROUND

The first stage in teaching the horse to jump is to introduce poles on the ground. To start with I place them in various different spots around the school so that in the course of his normal work the horse will learn to work over the poles in a relaxed manner whilst keeping a constant rhythm, no matter what pace he is in. In this way he has to think for himself where to put his feet right from the outset. If he resists, be firm but quiet, using your legs and making sure you maintain the rein contact. Until he is completely happy and relaxed working over poles, without altering his rhythm, there is no point in going on to the next stage.

Gradually I will introduce more equally spaced poles, between 3 and 4ft (1–1.2m) apart depending on the length of the horse's stride in trot. These should be far enough apart so he has to learn to open his shoulder slightly and use his hocks but not so far that he has to add extra strides and shuffle through them. It is a great exercise not only as jumping preparation but also for improving the horse's general trotwork, and helping you to fix the all-important trot rhythm in your head.

Another good exercise for horses at all levels, if you are working in a school, is to place a couple of poles on a large circle, one on each side, and a couple more placed four or five strides apart up the long side of the school. With poles positioned like this I work in canter, really concentrating on the quality and rhythm so I meet each pole in a balanced fashion, and again the horse learns to stay relaxed. As he becomes more established you can start adjusting the canter so the horse learns to lengthen and shorten his stride, so between poles you can add or take out strides while still maintaining the balance and rhythm.

CROSSPOLES AND SINGLE FENCES

It is up to you whether you place a trotting pole in front of the fence to begin with. I usually start with a little crosspole on its own, so that the horse only has to concentrate on the one element. When he is confidently jumping the crosspole, I put up a small vertical. I continue to jump from trot, but allow the horse to break into canter on landing.

The next stage is to ask the horse to jump a small crosspole out of trot. As the horse has been taught with his flatwork, he must go forward and in front of the leg. The rider must be quick to have their leg on if they feel the horse backing off, and must be ready to straighten the horse if he tries to run out.

⋀ **TROTTING POLES:** A useful exercise for helping to maintain a rhythm is to work the horse over poles on the ground, gradually building up to working in trot over five or six in a row 3–4ft (1–1.2m) apart (*left*). In canter I count every time

the horse takes a stride (*centre*); if my counting slows or quickens, I know the rhythm isn't established. The horse should learn to lengthen or shorten his stride while maintaining the rhythm as he canters over the poles. Note how the

horse meets the pole incorrectly (*right*) when you push him out of that steady rhythm. Using the poles not only helps the horse to concentrate on what he is doing but it is a great exercise for helping you to develop your own eye

⋎ **SIMPLE CROSSPOLE:** The rider should have the horse going forward and in front of the leg and be ready for him to back off. Note how I have released my fingers, thus allowing the horse freedom to use his neck

Learning to enjoy it

All horses progress at different rates and you must play it by ear in an early jumping session; but most will enjoy it and associate jumping with fun. The greener horses will need more time and understanding, but the bolder ones mustn't be held back and should be allowed to do as much as they enjoy. Beware of helping the young horse too much at a fence: you can't hope to meet every fence right, and it's important that he works out for himself how to organise his legs. If he hits a fence it is always interesting to see what his reaction will be when he is asked to jump the next one: a naturally careful horse will back *himself* off the next fence, while the bolder type must learn to do this. But by this, I don't mean backing off and dropping behind the leg. Whichever type he is, the point is that the horse has to learn to think for himself.

The next stage, when the horse is confidently jumping single fences around the school, is to go back to the crosspole with a trotting pole placed on the ground as the first step toward building up a grid. I then put up a second fence after the crosspole – I usually make it a vertical; I approach in trot, so I am not tempted to interfere with the horse, but then let him canter on to the next one.

➤ **JUMPING OUT OF CANTER:** I find jumping four-year-olds out of canter to be a good discipline for me because you mustn't interfere with them; they can't hold a shorter, balanced canter because they aren't strong enough, so you must let them jump from a more forward canter which they can hold naturally

➤ **CROSSPOLE and VERTICAL:** Placing a pole on the ground between the two elements encourages the horse to look down and use his head, neck and back over a fence. This is useful for horses that tend to rush or hollow when jumping

VARYING THE FENCES

With a helper on the ground who can raise fences and build other ones, I will ride the youngster over a variety of fences – uprights, crosspoles, fences with fillers and airy, upright poles – in canter so that he gains confidence, doesn't have time to think about mucking about, and enjoys it.

Try using a small filler fence flat on the ground so that it imitates a ditch. Approach in trot the first time to reduce the likelihood of a run out, and to maintain greater control. If he stops, which a youngster quite often does because he is alarmed by the sight of this new obstacle, don't worry! Just straightaway come again at the same speed, being stronger with your legs, and be ready with a defensive seat for a horrible awkward cat-jump! Repeat this until he jumps the filler confidently, and always reward him afterwards.

GRIDWORK

The idea of gridwork, a line of jumps in the school, is to develop the horse's athleticism and shape over fences, making him jump off his hocks and pick up his front legs. Gridwork also lets the rider really concentrate on their position and balance. I would not make initial gridwork for the youngster too demanding, keeping things simple and only adding extra fences as the horse became more confident. For a first lesson I would not incorporate a bounce, for instance.

You can build a variety of grids to improve a horse's technique or just to get him really thinking for himself. It is a case of deciding what exercises could help improve your young horse. For example, if I have a horse that is not very accurate with its front legs or is difficult to keep straight I build a grid of crosspoles. I start with a ground pole followed by a crosspole, then I add another crosspole at one stride's distance, then maybe a cross oxer off one or two strides. As the horse gains confidence I raise the crosspoles; the higher they are the sharper and tighter he has to make his front limb technique.

For a horse that hollows through his back and does not use his head and neck, place poles on the ground between each element. Looking at these encourages him to drop his head.

Gridwork can be hugely beneficial but these gymnastic exercises can also be tiring so don't overdo it. Use gridwork as well as your normal jumping sessions, not instead of them, and don't neglect to practise jumping courses out of a balanced canter.

TROUBLESHOOTING

My horse is overbold and rushes, what do I do?

This can sometimes be a result of lack of confidence or because the horse has not yet learned to come to a fence in a consistent rhythm. It can be useful to go back to basics and get him cantering quietly over poles on a related distance so he is concentrating and keeping his rhythm, but not anticipating a fence. Another good exercise is to place two crosspoles on a four- or five-stride related distance. Every time the horse gains speed or tries to rush, put him on a circle, left if he is on the left lead and right if on the right lead – the aim is to make the whole exercise as smooth as possible. When he is relaxed jump the fence, but if he seriously rushes, pull him up straight away and fairly smartly if necessary. You may have to be quite strong with your hand the first time, but as soon as he is standing pat him and then come again. Try to avoid pulling him away from a fence on the last stride because that will just teach him to run out.

My horse knocks down fences and is careless.

First ask yourself if he really *is* careless, or if there is another reason: does he knock them because he is going hollow? Rushing? Popping in an extra stride on approach? Check your riding: perhaps you are hanging on to the reins too much, catching him in the mouth, rocking about in the saddle – *you* may be causing the problem. Check that nothing is hurting the horse: his mouth or teeth, his back, his feet, the tack – any of these can affect how tidily he jumps. He may be tired: perhaps you have schooled him for too long, made the exercises too hard for his stage of training, maybe he is just not mature enough to cope yet. If he is truly careless, try setting up a grid with short distances between the fences, and use 'V' poles (see page 92) to make him bring his knees up more sharply and be snappier behind. Ride him in a short, bouncy canter in a regular rhythm so he can make full use of the power in his quarters when he actually jumps – if you let him get too long, or 'fire' him at his fences, he is almost bound to knock them down.

How do I stop my horse from running out?

First establish *why* he is running out: with a young horse, maybe you are asking too much of him – it may be a lack of confidence, perhaps you have made the fences too high or spooky; or he may be tired. Ensure your schooling sessions are not too long or taxing. Check nothing hurts: his back, feet, teeth or tack: he won't enjoy jumping if something is painful. If you are sure that his evasion is just naughtiness you will need to be firm with him to sort this problem out. It's actually more difficult to cure a horse that consistently runs out than a horse that stops. If your horse runs out you must turn him immediately in the opposite direction, if he runs out to the left you must turn him right, and vice versa, before you then present him at the fence again. You must be absolutely sure that you have him channelled in front of your leg, with a secure rein contact. Right up to the point of take-off keep him in that 'tunnel' between your hands and legs so he can't escape to either side. Keep him straight and the instant you feel him start to drift, for example to the left, use your right rein and left leg to correct him. If your horse has had a run out or he is often inclined to run one way make sure you have your whip in that hand.

⋏ ⋗ JUMPING AT ANGLES: Horses have to learn that they must expect any sort of fence at any time, because this is what they will need to cope with when going cross country. Similarly the fences might come at awkward angles and difficult strides in a jump-off against the clock. Therefore at a fairly early stage I will practise turning the horse in tight to a fence, or asking him to jump on an angle. I might jump the exit fence of a double, but never just the first element as that could encourage a run-out

⋖ VARYING THE FENCES: The young horse needs to be introduced to all types of fence. Vary the order in which you jump them so he will learn to be prepared for any eventuality

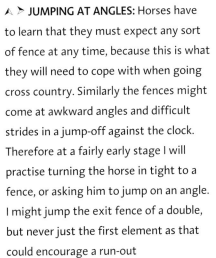

Training for accuracy

When you start jumping a horse it is essential that he is made to jump in the middle of a fence. This may seem obvious but is not always that easy. There are various reasons why the horse does not jump straight: the rider might be crooked, the horse himself could be crooked on the approach or falling out through one shoulder, or the horse might just always drift one way to give himself more room to take off. Whatever the reason it needs addressing. A good exercise for helping the horse to stay in the middle of his fences is to place poles in a V shape on the fence as shown.

⅄ USING 'V' POLES: Matter of Fact does normally jump straight – as you can see in the photograph (*below left*) – when the poles are slightly apart but when the poles are brought closer together he drifts to the right to avoid hitting them with his off fore. At the age of five he is not too accurate in front and so I am using this exercise to improve his front limb technique

TROUBLESHOOTING

My horse doesn't cover enough ground between fences in a combination.

This may be lack of confidence or physical immaturity, or you may have a short-striding horse or one that is behind your leg. It is important that the horse learns to put in the right number of strides in a combination. Don't interfere with him and never try to add extra strides, whether at home or in competition. If your horse is short-striding you will have to approach combinations with greater impulsion – though this doesn't mean gallop senselessly into them! Often a very green horse will slip in an extra stride simply because he has momentarily lost impulsion, stood off the first element, then jumped big and landed short. He will then find it hard to make up the distance to the next part. To avoid this make sure he is in front of your leg and be

quick on landing to encourage him forward to the next element, keeping your body in balance. If you get ahead of the movement your legs won't have any affect.

My horse backs off his fences, especially a double.

This is probably lack of experience; lack of confidence in his rider; or because he is naturally spooky, or careful. Use simple, easy grids to build up his confidence: ground poles to a couple of crosspoles with one stride (20–23ft [6–7m]) in between, and when he does this happily, add a third crosspole or simple upright a two-stride distance (36ft [11m]) away; if he does this all right, move it to a stride (20–23ft [6–7m]) away. This will help him get used to coping with a line of jumps. You must be quick to put your leg on firmly if he backs off, and keep a steady, constant rein contact if he wobbles as he approaches.

Exercises for athleticism

MOCK CROSS-COUNTRY FENCES

A useful precursor to cross-country training is building show jumps into angles in a mock version of cross-country fences. You can get the young horse used to being obedient about narrow fences and corners. He will learn to jump where you tell him to, and if you jump the fences at different angles and in different directions, he will learn to jump off turns and to change legs and, therefore, to balance.

Building knock-down fences into the shape of mock cross-country fences, such as angled rails, arrowheads, corners and coffins will educate the youngster while making jumping sessions more interesting. They will teach him how to cope with these before he is asked to jump the same shapes but in solid construction, and they will teach the rider to keep the horse straight.

All my basic preparation for cross-country jumping takes place in the school, and I wouldn't think of taking a youngster cross-country schooling over solid fences until I felt he was confident, balanced and safe over jumps that knock down!

➤ **MOCK ARROWHEAD:** As with the corner you must keep the horse channelled between your legs and into an even rein contact. It helps to have some jumping poles cut to a variety of lengths so you don't have to start off with a very narrow target. As your horse builds confidence and grasps the idea of staying on the right line, the wings can be moved closer together so that you have less and less to aim at. Next you can replace the 'face' of the arrowhead with a slightly narrower pole.

I find it amazing how quickly a young horse gets the hang of jumping both corners and arrowheads but his training does need to be taken gradually. You cannot expect him to jump a 2ft (60cm) wide arrowhead or barrel straight off, without building up to it. This would be the quickest way to teach him to run out

◁ **MOCK CORNER:** Having worked at keeping the horse in the middle of a fence, and then having got him used to the idea of jumping fences on an angle, you will now be ready for your first corner. In preparation I start with just a single upright and oxer, and practise jumping over a precise part of a fence. If you've got striped poles aim for a certain stripe making sure the horse is channelled down a 'corridor' towards it. When you introduce your first small corner it will be no different from your precision jumping of the oxer. Be aware that, even though the corner is small and narrow, you must be accurate and jump the exact point you have chosen to jump. If you can keep the horse on a precise line he will have no problem when you start making the corner larger and wider

8

Cross-country schooling

So much of cross-country success is due to confidence. The aim of early schooling over small cross-country fences is to get the young horse to trust the rider that whatever he is asked to do is all right.

The foundations for cross-country will have been laid when out hacking. When out for a ride, I never avoid natural 'hazards', but encourage a horse to go straight through puddles, to jump small logs in woods and to negotiate small natural features such as banks, ditches, muddy bridlepaths, undulations and branches on the ground where the horse has to work out for himself where his feet should go.

If the initial flatwork has been carried out correctly and the horse has learned to come off the leg, this will save many problems when you start cross-country. By the time I take a youngster cross-country schooling – usually when he is either coming towards the end of his four-year-old year or at the start of his five-year-old year, depending on the weather and his development – he will be jumping in an established way over coloured poles, perhaps having been to a few small competitions. He will have been schooled over 'mock' cross-country fences made of coloured poles (see pages 94 and 95) and will have an improved natural balance and know where to put his feet.

Aims of schooling

When cross-country schooling, my aim as a rider is, believe it or not, to do as little as possible. The idea is that the horse works out for himself what to do. It is a paradox that one of the problems – dangers, even – of eventing is that because the dressage phase has become so influential – in that however well you jump, if your dressage mark isn't good, you have small hope of doing well – riders risk over-training horses to the point that they are waiting for our every command. The horse must keep his ability to think for himself so that he can get out of trouble when the rider can't be there for him; for instance if he leaves a leg behind in a combination fence and tips the rider off balance, he will probably have to negotiate the next part of the fence without a lot of help from his rider.

No horse can be foot-perfect at every fence, and inevitably there will be the occasional missed stride or leg left behind. When riding a youngster, the problems are accentuated because they might suddenly spook or jink on approach to a fence and the rider can find themselves in completely the wrong position. It is, therefore, essential to keep your leg on and remain slightly behind the movement, allowing the horse the freedom to sort it out for himself.

THINKING ABOUT TACK

I try to keep everything simple. **Bridles:** I stick to using a plain snaffle bridle but I do have a large selection – rubber snaffles, Fulmers, French links, plain single-jointed, the list goes on. With fancy bits the list is shorter; the only bits that I ride stronger horses in when going cross-country are a large, loose-ringed rubber gag or a Waterford Fulmer. I don't play around with complicated bits because I think problems of control generally stem from inside the horse's head. I use rubber reins – there is nothing worse than reins that slip, particularly when wet or sweaty. A flash noseband is my preference, but incorrectly fitting a noseband risks obstructing the horse's breathing and causing it pain. I use a running martingale but adjust it so there is no danger of it restricting the horse, and I also have a breastplate. **Saddles:** I use Devoucoux, a French saddle: both the dressage and jumping saddles are close contact, and the leather is very soft. I tend to use Polypad numnahs as they seem to wash well and offer the horse's back plenty of protection. **Boots:** I use open-fronted tendon boots and fetlock boots behind for the show jumping, and back boots plus overreach boots for cross-country, all made by Devoucoux.

➤ **PRE-SCHOOLING TRAINING:** Iceman jumping his first steeplechase fence at racehorse trainer Guy Harwood's Coombelands Farm

Preparation and warm-up

Always go cross-country schooling with company, including someone on a more experienced horse who can give your first-timer a lead and thus avoid confrontations at hazards such as water and ditches.

As I have emphasised before, I will do anything to avoid an argument with the young horse – though having said that, when cross-country schooling, you must still be prepared to make him do what is asked. For instance, even if a horse is adamant it won't go over a ditch, I will stay there and make it do so, even if it takes hours. It is vital that a horse doesn't go home having got away with refusing to do what is asked, or he will be forever in charge in your relationship. Often you will hear people say, 'my horse won't jump ditches' and it is for no other reason than that their horse has been allowed to get away with misbehaving.

You might find that your youngster, faced with the exciting wide open space of a cross-country course, will be quite bright. Make sure you have a helper who can give you a good clean leg-up, and if you feel the horse may be about to rush forward, face him towards something solid, like the side of a building or a fence. Make sure your girth is tight enough before you get on and that your stirrups are the right length, because if the horse is lively, you won't have time to adjust them in the first few minutes of being on his back.

TROUBLESHOOTING

The importance of rewarding the young horse

It is really vital always to reassure and reward the young horse, even as he is tackling a hazard. For instance, if he gets stuck at a ditch or at water, give frequent kicks and little taps with the whip as long as he is running back, napping out to the side, or generally refusing to go. But the instant he lowers his head to have a look or a sniff, take a step forward, or you feel that his attitude has changed and he is thinking about going, then you must be immediately ready to pat him and encourage/reward him with your voice and by easing the reins. You will have to be quick in doing this: one minute you will be kicking/tapping, the next patting/rewarding.

How do I cope with the over-excited horse?

If the horse feels as though he would like to buck, get him into a brisk trot, ride him forward and sit safely behind the movement with your leg forward. Horses often feel like a coiled spring on these occasions, especially if it is cold weather. The worst thing you can do is to pull him up, because this will generally encourage him to muck about even more, so kick him on out of his naughtiness and keep him moving until you feel his back come down and he starts to relax. When he is settled, check your girth.

Warm-up fence

Trot and canter around for about ten minutes at the most, depending on how far you have hacked to get to the course. Remember that although the young horse must be warmed up, he won't be fit like an older horse, so don't wear him out before you've even begun jumping.

The first fence should be a small rail or log. Approach it in canter and pop over it in both directions a few times. If the horse feels green, keep repeating the exercise until he feels more confident and fluent. Then try and work out a simple route over three or four small, simple fences in sequence, working on keeping him in a quiet rhythm – speed is not an issue at this stage.

KEEP IT SIMPLE: Keep the early fences small and straightforward and your seat slightly behind the movement, as the first few attempts at jumping may be unpredictable. Sure enough, Iceman, who has backed off the tyres at first sight (*left*), overjumps and then attempts to put in a buck afterward (*above*). The second attempt (*sequence below*) shows a more settled approach and a happier expression on his face

Rider position

The important thing is to stay in balance with the horse, either in the centre of the movement or slightly behind it. Never get in front of the movement – this is the single most influential factor in causing problems. If your upper body is tipped forward and your lower legs have gone backwards, your weight will be thrown forward on to the horse's forehand, making it more difficult for him to balance himself, and you are much more likely to fall off if he stops suddenly or leaves a leg behind over a fence.

Different horses will canter and gallop in a different way and youngsters do tend to be more on their forehand. However, at this stage I don't worry about how they cover the ground. I try to focus the horse with my legs, always riding up into a secure contact, and try to get him in balance in front of a fence by closing my leg and taking my upper body back. This slight adjustment of position will engage the horse's hind end and bring the front up.

I play around with this exercise so that a consistent rhythm is maintained for the straightforward fences. The rider shouldn't be pulling on the horse's mouth to get his hocks underneath him; all it needs is an adjustment of bodyweight.

At the trickier combination fences, which will be tackled in later sessions, a shorter, bouncy canter is required on the approach, and it is important to establish the rhythm you want in plenty of time. Do not spend the last two or three strides interfering with the horse, but give

The ability to stay behind the movement by slipping the reins did not come naturally to me and I have had to work on it very hard over the years in order to transform my cross-country riding. Once I managed to do this, it made all the difference.

him the freedom to see what he has to do to get over the fence. Often you will see riders hooking their horse back too late so that in the last few strides they are trying to slow them with the hand, the horse is fighting for its head and doesn't get to see the fence until the last minute. This is when the horse is more likely to have a stop or leave a leg behind.

If the horse backs off a fence, encourage him forward with your legs rather than with your upper body, which will put you ahead of the movement. Be quiet but firm and don't flap your legs.

Try to sense what the horse is going to do – at this age they might do anything! – and be prepared for him to stop or run out. If, for instance, he runs out to the right, turn him to the left straightaway.

I like to think of the neck as being the horse's fifth leg. He must have the freedom to use his neck and head for balance when landing. When jumping drops, as he uses his neck open your fingers so he can take an extra length of the rein. This also prevents you from being pulled forward.

First bank/step down

Approach in trot and allow the horse plenty of time to eye up the obstacle ahead and work out what he has to do. Do not use speed to try to overcome what may be natural suspicion. Maintain the rein contact with his mouth, and keep the leg on. Ride on and off the bank at a variety of angles. Approach in canter, remaining behind the movement and being ready to open your fingers and feed an inch or so of rein, allowing the horse to use his head and neck to balance on landing. Don't throw the reins at him; maintain contact but allow freedom. If a horse doesn't have the freedom of his head and neck he will find it difficult to balance over drops, a problem many riders discover to their cost later on when negotiating a big drop into water.

FIRST STEP: Iceman's suspicion at this tiny step up on to a bank illustrates why first cross-country obstacles must be small and unthreatening. As he approaches he attempts to go sideways, but I keep urging him on, keeping him straight between my legs, and he jumps up neatly. Once on the bank, I try to keep him going, though allowing him a look,

before he steps off quite happily.
It is important that the rider does not
use speed to sort out this reluctance, for
the horse has to learn to look and work
out the task ahead for himself. The rider
should maintain contact with the horse's
mouth, feeding an inch or so of rein
down the step and keeping their leg on

A bigger bank/step down

MAKING PROGRESS: The smallness of the first step has given Iceman confidence and he shows only momentary hesitation at this slightly deeper version. You can see (*bottom right*) I have slipped my reins to allow him freedom of the head and neck, and I have remained behind the movement

CROSS-COUNTRY SCHOOLING

Combination rail to step down

The next stage is jumping a small log or rail on top of a bank before the step down. Again, allow the horse to look, keep your leg on and remain a fraction behind the movement.

If the horse is too bold and tends to jump too big off the step, come back and do it more quietly, checking the horse slightly on approach and then soften the hand on take-off. Repeat this exercise until the horse is more relaxed. Over-boldness at this stage can be a sign of a lack of confidence and is an issue which needs to be overcome now before tackling drops into water.

From your mock cross-country schooling (see previous chapter) you should have a feel for how naturally brave your horse is. If he is confident don't try and hold him back. He won't need to keep repeating the same obstacle over and over again.

⋎ **RAIL BEFORE A STEP:** Iceman is now happy to jump a rail before the step down, and is doing it easily. I concentrate on allowing him to have a look at what he is doing while keeping my leg on and remaining a fraction behind the movement so that I do not unbalance him

↘ **MAKING PROGRESS:** If you compare these pictures to the ones on p106, you can see how quickly Iceman has gained confidence and realised it's meant to be fun

TROUBLESHOOTING

What if my horse becomes too strong?

Your horse may be strong if he is either overbold or lacks confidence, this is why (as with showjump schooling) it's important to maintain a steady, regular rhythm between fences. The worst thing you can do is to keep pulling as this just encourages the horse to pull back. Remember that this problem is more often than not an issue of the brain, not the mouth, so don't resort to using a more severe bit. If with continuous training you still find your horse is too strong, you may have to weigh up the possibility that he is not suitable for you. I would never think about competing a horse cross-country if I didn't have control.

Ditches

This is one of the hazards a young horse is likely to find most frightening – 95 per cent of young horses will have a good gawp at their first ditch. It is also highly likely that he will either stop, whip round or run out, and it is important not to let him get away with it; make sure that he is jumping backward and forward over the ditch by the end of the session confidently, because if he isn't 100 per cent happy at this stage, you could have problems forever.

Like everything else, the secret is to keep the horse in front of the leg, edging him forward. Again, it is important that you allow him to have a look and see what he has to jump, and to work out what he should do with his legs, so approach in trot as this will make him easier to control.

Be prepared for the horse to stop dead and then balloon over the ditch, which can be uncomfortable and unbalancing for the rider. Nevertheless, it is important not to catch him in the mouth, so be ready.

Some riders consider you should ride at a ditch as if it isn't there. I agree with this if the ditch is sited on the take-off side of a fence, because these are basically designed to be rider-frighteners and the horses will be quick to pick up from the rider that there is a problem ahead. Sometimes a rider will get nervous about the ditch and over-ride, pushing the horse out of balance and making him suspicious as he wonders why he is being harassed. Instead, keep the horse in front of your leg and stay in a positive rhythm without trying to get to the fence too quickly.

DITCH: (*opposite, bottom left and centre*) Iceman shows typical inexperience in his resistance at the sight of his first ditch, and tries to run out. This was partly because I had presented him in canter, so when I had got him under control again and re-presented him in trot (*opposite top and left*) I managed to keep him straighter

However, he still kept looking at the ditch and backing off, so I knew I would have an uncomfortable jump over it (*main picture and above*) and kept my leg forward so that I was ready for it and did not catch him in the mouth

Trakehner

➤ **GAINING COURAGE:** (*sequence right*) Iceman was soon quite confident about jumping ditches, and later in the schooling session was happy to jump a small fence with a ditch underneath. He backed off it slightly, but I kept him straight between my leg and hand and he jumped it well

◁ ⋏ **SECOND ATTEMPT:** Here he shows an altogether more confident approach. I am sitting up and keeping him straight, and as a result he jumps boldly but neatly

TROUBLESHOOTING

My horse refuses to jump ditches. What should I do?

Occasionally I have had a horse who has taken a major dislike to ditches and won't even accept a lead from another horse. In those circumstances I have kept him facing square on to the ditch and kept edging him forward. If he really won't move, I would use the whip, but only as a last resort.

Some horses can be very stubborn about ditches and I have known one who used to switch off mentally on approach. He was the most difficult, as he would go numb on the leg and wouldn't respond. The eventual answer was to summon help and have two people standing one on each side of him with a lunge whip.

It may seem hard on the horse and I absolutely hate doing it, but it is essential to win this battle. If you lose the argument and give up, the horse will always take advantage of his rider in the future. Keep a cool head; never lose your temper. When the horse eventually jumps the ditch, reward him in exaggerated fashion and then come straight round and jump it again. Do this until he is jumping the ditch happily and confidently.

Getting used to water

Always have a lead at hand for the first time a horse is ridden into water because, as with ditches, it is important to try and avoid a conflict. A young horse cannot be expected to know that it is all right to go into water for the first time: at this stage he doesn't know the rider well enough to trust him/her, he doesn't know how deep the water is, or if the footing is safe.

To begin with, walk the horse into the water if you can, keeping him quietly channelled between your leg and hand; if he is not going to go on his own, follow the lead horse in. Spend some time walking him around in the water so that he realises there is nothing to be worried about.

Repeat the exercise, this time without a lead, and then at trot. Vary the direction you go in and out and introduce small jumps before and after the water.

BE READY FOR THE UNEXPECTED:
Matter Of Fact (Matty) proves the point that youngsters are totally unpredictable, for he had previously jumped the small ditches without hesitation and I imagined that he would be similarly unperturbed about water. However, instead he resisted and then 'froze'

After I gave him a smack with the whip and got him facing straight, Matty followed the lead horse (ridden by Iceman's owner, Jonathan Ford) into the water, for which I made sure to reward him. After that he splashed around happily and I made a great fuss of him

Steps out of water

Steps out of water can cause as many problems as jumping in, but at this stage the rider must just do their best to keep the horse balanced by keeping the leg on and then just nudge him up the steps. Having slipped the reins on entering the water, be prepared to take up the slack quickly as you land so that you have a steady contact and can support him if necessary as he jumps out. If there is no time to shorten the reins, be prepared to take your arms back to take up the slack.

During the schooling session, be alert to how tired the young horse is getting: he may run out of energy quite quickly, and this is when accidents happen and confidence is lost. If you feel him flagging, stop the session. Above all, cross-country schooling should be fun for both horse and rider. Reward him continually and keep him busy; as long as they are not over-faced, horses usually really enjoy cross-country schooling and their confidence and agility grows astonishingly fast.

▽ **MORE CONFIDENT:** Having realised there is now nothing to be frightened of, Matter of Fact lives up to his name and is more than happy to trot through the water

RAPID PROGRESS: The water exercise is repeated happily in canter, demonstrating that once a young horse's confidence is won, he will progress quickly; you can see by the expression on Matty's face that he is now really enjoying it

Jumping into water

The main problem with young horses and water is over-jumping into it, and the same principles apply as for steps down.

As a youngster, Teddy Twilight was incredibly bold in water and always approached with a 'let me at it' attitude. At his second intermediate competition the drop into water was a lot bigger than he was used to; he over-jumped and was unable to get his landing gear down in time, resulting in a harmless, but very smelly fall. This shook him, but it taught him a lesson, and straightaway I took him schooling into a similar water fence, making him jump through it more quietly. Even now if I come to a rail two strides before water with him, I will get him back to trot and make him pop in quietly rather than jumping from canter.

Do not underestimate the drag effect that water can have on a horse's stride. Even over an apparently standard distance it is difficult to predict exactly how many strides he will take in water, so be prepared for the occasional awkward jump out.

BOLD AS BRASS: Despite Iceman's initial aversion to ditches, he was as bold as brass into water and was soon cantering in over a small rail and jumping out neatly. I have slipped my reins jumping into the water, taking up the slack as we progress through the water with my leg on, nudging him towards the step; he is coping well with the dragging feeling of cantering through water. The pictures below and right show a good example of getting in front of the movement, but I am quick to get my balance back (*far right*) for the next element

More advanced cross-country

PROGRESS CHECK

Before you move on to more advanced cross-country fences there are a few points that you need to be sure of:

Is your horse happy to:

• stay in a good, regular rhythm over a succession of simple cross-country fences?
• jump into and out of water?
• jump a small ditch?
• jump up and down a small step or bank?

Can your horse:

• stay balanced jumping a course of small cross-country fences?
• tackle ditches, steps and water confidently, without being spooky or nappy?

I cannot emphasise enough the main ingredient for a good, safe cross-country horse is confidence. The trust you will build and the enjoyment you will share comes from that confidence, hence it is vitally important that you do not try and run before you can walk. I have made this point on many occasions throughout this book, so you should be able to assess when your horse is happy and ready to progress to the slightly more demanding questions that will be asked of him next.

It does help if your horse has met all the various types of fences and hazards in training before he gets to his first event, it's better to be over prepared than under prepared. I also find it essential to give the more experienced horses some cross-country schooling if they have lost a bit of confidence, or just before the start of the season. For them these schooling days are not meant to be testing, but just an opportunity to give them fun and a bit of a 'jolly'. I for one would not be able to school over any fences above intermediate level in cold blood.

At the end of this stage if you feel you and your young horse have really enjoyed it and he is coping happily with whatever he is asked, then he should be ready for his first event. If not, he might need a few more schooling days.

The bounce fence

While you wouldn't necessarily find a bounce on every pre-novice course, they do crop up sometimes and will certainly feature at novice level, so this is something I would teach a five-year-old.

It is important to establish the correct pace early enough so that in the last two or three strides before the fence, the rider is able to ride forward and let the horse work out what he has got to do. Stay sitting up and engage the horse's back end from the forward canter as you do in all jumping. (Remember: it is our job to approach the fence correctly and the horse's job to jump it when it gets there.)

If you go too fast and then suddenly try to kill the speed at the last minute, the horse will get its head up in the air and not be able to see what it is jumping, resulting in an awkward jump and possible mistakes.

TROUBLESHOOTING

My horse tries to put in a stride, or stops at the second element: what am I doing wrong?

Probably you haven't established a strong enough forward canter, so your horse hasn't the impulsion to jump the second part of the bounce. This doesn't necessarily mean faster: you should use more leg whilst keeping a steady rein contact to contain the energy your leg creates, and this will generate more power and bounce in the horse's canter stride (rather than the speed). Practise bounces in the school: build a grid with bounces (10ft[3m]) in it, crosspoles to start with, then building up to 2ft 6in (76cm) uprights; then tackle a bounce on its own, all the time concentrating on how strong a canter you need in order to jump it fluently. Perhaps you are nervous about bounces, and are hanging on by the reins: whilst it is important to maintain a contact, be sure you are allowing the horse forward, and not holding the reins too tight.

My horse throws his head around coming into a bounce, and generally catches a front leg: what am I doing wrong?

You are probably leaving it too late to slow him down, and pulling him with your hand to steady and/or correct his line. A bounce is difficult for the horse to judge if he is into his stride going across country, and it is important to steady him and set him up early enough so he is approaching in a show-jumping type canter, round and bouncy, and not too fast and flat at steeplechase speed. So sit up, balance him, get his hocks under him, and try to come in close to the first element, rather than standing off it – but keep the leg on and ride forward in the last two or three strides so he has the impulsion to jump the second element well.

⋏ **RIDING A BOUNCE:** Jurassic Rising, a horse I have had since he was a baby, tackles a bounce fence during a session at Eddy Stibbe's cross-country schooling course at Waresley Park. Jurassic Rising is now competing at three-star level and is familiar with bounce fences. He is having a look at the obstacle, but I have kept my leg on and have not got ahead of the movement

The corner

Nowadays, accuracy and being able to stay true to your line through a combination or over a fence such as a corner, are a huge part of cross-country riding and the corner is very much a typical test of that. While jumping knock-down versions of the corner in the school, the youngster needs to learn to jump normally and not to one side. Then the principle is the same with both corners and arrowheads and, in fact, all narrow fences: the idea is to feel that the horse is locked in a channel between your legs and hands and cannot run out. If you have got the horse properly in this 'channel', you will feel when he might lose straightness and will be in a position to keep him on the line you have chosen.

CORNERS: Jurassic Rising has seen many corners before, but you can just see that he is slightly drifting out through his right shoulder on approach (*left*), so I am keeping hold of the left rein and have my right leg on to make sure that he stays on the line I am asking him to hold

TROUBLESHOOTING

I am nervous about landing in the middle of a corner: how can I best judge it to jump safely?

Think of the corner as a triangle, and imagine a straight line from the point of the V to the middle of the base line of the triangle; if you are straight, you will be approaching this straight line at 90 degrees. Keep as near to the point as you dare, without risking a run out, where the angle is narrowest, but always keeping at 90 degrees to your imaginary straight line. Like the bounce fence, establish a short, bouncy show-jumping canter well before the fence so you can ride forward for the last two or three strides; this will make sure the horse's hocks are well underneath him, to guarantee a safe jump.

My horse always runs out at a corner: what am I doing wrong?

Riding a corner successfully demands a great deal of control – you can't rely on speed to keep you straight and on a line. You are probably coming in without enough impulsion – either too fast and flat, or too slow so the horse is wavery and hard to keep on your line. Again, you must have him at a pace in which you have plenty of control and he is really between your hand and leg, in a shorter, show-jumping type of canter – though make sure you come in strongly and keep coming forward for the last two or three approach strides. Try not to overcheck and hold on to his head too much – the horse will lose his rhythm and momentum coming in to a fence, and will start to think backward, and once this happens it is easy for him to run out.

The arrowhead

Another test of accuracy which requires the horse to be ridden down that 'channel'. Do not be tempted to loosen your contact on the last stride. Again, do not even think about the possibility of a run-out, but maintain, with quiet determination, the feeling that the horse is completely channelled between your hand and leg and has to jump at the central point you ask him to.

ARROWHEADS: In these pictures, where Jurassic Rising is jumping at an arrowhead with one stride to a rail, my rider position is, if anything, slightly behind the movement, but it can never be emphasised too often that when riding across country the rider should never be in front of the movement. He is having a bit of a look (*left, top*), but as he has no choice in the matter, negotiates the complex with confidence

TROUBLESHOOTING

I find it really hard to aim my horse straight at narrow fences: how do I improve this?

The less a horse is going forward, the harder he is to keep straight, so probably your canter is not strong and forward enough; you may also be trying to correct him and keep him 'on line' by using your hands, rather than holding and directing him with your leg. Check your body position, and make sure you are not tipping your upper body too far forward: this will make it harder for you to use your legs with any influence. Also when you walk a course – and you should do this when cross-country schooling, too – work out exactly the line of approach you are going to take, and exactly where you are going to jump the fence: then when you come to ride it, you will do so positively.

I worry when I can't see a stride into a fence, especially a tricky one like an arrowhead: how can I learn to do this?

Keep the leg on and 'hold' (maintain the contact on his mouth) so the horse shortens and makes two strides in a short distance; or squeeze and slightly ease the rein so he covers a bit more ground and stands off a little. For 'accuracy' fences it is often better to hold and shorten – and this does not mean haul him in the teeth and forget about your legs! It means almost more leg so he really gets his hocks under him and 'concertinas' into a rounder shape – then even if he gets under a fence a bit, he is still able to jump up and out over it. The worse thing you can do is chuck the reins at him and 'fire' him at it, when he is likely to throw his head up and run at it; like this he will lose his balance, and you will have no hope of keeping him straight.

Triple brush

This is another increasingly common type of accuracy question similar to the arrowhead. Obviously the triple brush is a more difficult fence because it has no wing of any sort and, therefore, keeping the horse channelled is even more important to keep him 'on track'. Again, many riders make the mistake of approaching too fast in an effort to prevent the horse running out but, in fact, they end up with less control should the horse be disobedient.

Drop log

With this type of fence, it is important to balance the horse at the bottom of the preceding slope and ride him firmly up the mound to the log. On the point of take-off, keep the leg on but feed a little bit of rein through your fingers to prepare for the drop and sit up, rather than leaning forwards, so that you will have a better chance of landing in balance and therefore helping your horse to stay in balance.

The principle with all drop fences is that the horse needs the freedom of its head and neck as a 'fifth leg'. This is why being able to slip the reins is such an important rider skill, which I must admit to having found very difficult at first. It will also give you a better chance to avoid flopping forward if the horse pecks or stumbles.

TRUSTING HIS RIDER: This log had an uphill approach and a downhill landing so that as the horse takes off he can't see what is on the other side, so it is important to ride with confidence. Here I am ready with my leg to react if he backs off

Coffin

The coffin can be a deceptively difficult exercise although you will often find in competition that the challenge is reduced because a rounded, rather than upright obstacle is used as the first element of the fence. Even so, it needs to be approached with a shorter, more active canter, which reduces the speed as you come into the fence. This needs to be established early in your approach so that you can put your leg on in the last two or three strides, ensuring enough impulsion to clear the first element. Remember that the horse needs time to look at the question so never gallop into a coffin: if you do, you will risk the horse not seeing the ditch, giving him no time to work out what to do with his legs.

DECEPTIVELY DIFFICULT: This coffin has an uphill approach and, on landing downhill, the horse is confronted by a ditch, although here the test has been softened by a more forgiving, rounded log on approach. For this reason I am slightly behind the movement over the first element because Jurassic Rising, as anticipated, is having a good look and I encourage him with my leg. If I was being particularly critical, I would say I've got slightly in front of the movement (*opposite bottom left*) but by the next picture you can see that I've managed to shift my weight behind the horse again

TROUBLESHOOTING

As soon as my horse sees the ditch he stops dead

Go schooling over ditches! Your number one priority in any stage of training is that the horse goes forward from the leg, and that he gets to the other side of the fence. It is therefore very important that you don't overface him, and expect him to tackle something that is too difficult either for his courage, or his stage of training. Horses often seem to find a coffin tricky, so choose a schooling course where there is a small one, with a not-too-wide ditch, and at least a couple of strides (36ft [12m]) between the jumping elements and the ditch. Then jump it in stages: first just the ditch and exit fence – you may have to angle it a bit so as to avoid the 'in' jump – and only when he is happy with this should you attempt the whole combination.

My horse pops in extra strides through a coffin, resulting in an awkward cat jump: should I go faster?

Not necessarily – it depends on the layout of the combination, and whether your horse has a long or a short stride. You should know how long his stride is from building grids in your show-jumping training, whether 20 or 26ft (6m or 8m) is a comfortable one-stride distance for him. So when you walk a cross-country course establish whether the distance between each element is long, short, or just right for your horse, and ride accordingly: more strongly for a short stride, or in a contained fashion for a long stride. Gradient makes a difference, too: uphill his stride shortens, downhill it will be longer. Also bear in mind that as he gains experience he will cover more ground and jump better.

Steps

Especially with steeper steps, I tend to drop the horse back to a trot for the approach. However, he should not be allowed to drop behind the leg and bit, so keep your leg on and, as for a drop, feed him the reins so that he can use his head and neck to help him balance himself.

If you allow a horse to come too strongly into steps they may either bound off them too bravely or be so surprised when they suddenly see the drop down that they stop dead. This is why it is important to get the horse back into a collected canter or trot so the rider is ready to squeeze them off the steps.

KEEP BEHIND THE MOVEMENT: In these pictures I am sitting, correctly, behind the movement and feeding the rein to the horse while still maintaining contact. If a horse is hesitant going down steps, the rider can easily be tipped forward up the neck, thereby increasing their chances of falling off

LOG INTO WATER

The same theory applies as with steps down. In the photographs below I have my leg on for the approach so I'm ready if Jurassic Rising decides he doesn't want to go. Again, do not get ahead of the movement, and be prepared to slip your reins so that you don't tip forward over his neck.

The pictures above show how I have allowed the reins to slip so that Jurassic Rising can really use his head and neck to balance. Note that although my reins are quite long, I am still maintaining a contact.

Double of logs into water

SLIPPING THE REINS: Jurassic Rising is happy enough at this double of logs into water. Keep a horse cantering forward at this sort of fence so that he doesn't lose impulsion when he sees the water. As with the steps down (pages 134-135), this sequence shows the horse having to use his head and neck on landing to balance himself. Again, think of the neck as the 'fifth leg'. Note that I keep my position secure (*centre, middle and bottom*) before picking up rein contact

⌄ **COPING WITH DRAG:** When schooling a youngster in water, let him have a bit of a play and splash so that he sees water is not a frightening thing, and that it has a reliable surface.

Water obviously affects a horse's natural stride because it causes a drag. If you can't get your horse to canter through water, don't worry. It doesn't bother me if he prefers to stay in trot in water, but if there is a fence out of the water, whether you are in trot or canter, it is more important to keep the impulsion level up and keep him going forward through it than the actual pace

PROGRESS CHECK

You will know from your schooling sessions how bold your horse is, and will be able to judge when he is confident and ready for his first competition. Check off the following list to be certain. The last thing you want is to be eliminated, which would mean leaving the course on a fall or refusal and storing up trouble for the future.

Has your horse:

• Learned to shorten or lengthen his stride to cope with tricky combinations?

• Overcome any wariness of ditches and water?

• Met each of the types of fence he is likely to need to cope with in his first competition at least once?

• Consistently and confidently jumped round several cross-country schooling courses?

9

First competitions

As in every stage with a young horse, preparation is the key. I try not to compete a youngster for the first time without having taken him to visit a competition just to have a look around and soak up the environment. It is too much to expect him to cope with all the other horses and the atmosphere – the flags, arenas, tents, loudspeakers and so on – and concentrate on competing successfully on top of that.

It really helps to be *over-prepared*. By this I mean that your horse should be capable of doing more than will be required of him in his first competition – more difficult dressage movements, and bigger fences. The challenge presented by the event or show should be reassuringly within his current level of training. You really don't want to be faced with a confrontation and an argument you can't win at this stage, and this means minimising the chance of a disheartening upset for both you and your horse at a first competition. If he has learned at home that work is fun and that he will be well rewarded for getting it right, then you are more likely to be rewarded by him going well in competition.

At the same time, don't expect too much too soon. Young horses often have a sense of humour and are extremely good at making the rider look very silly!

The first outing

I try to take all my four-year-olds to a small local show where I ride them around, work them in the warm-up area with other horses, and just sit and watch, taking care not to get in the way of *bona fide* competitors. Another idea is to take your youngster to a showground the day after a show, when the fences may still be up and the tents and flags still in place.

If he is travelling with a companion, part of the youngster's education is to be left in the horsebox on his own when the companion goes off to compete, but be prepared for him to be unsettled by this at first: don't just wander off vaguely, but use your common sense – make sure he can't hurt himself, and get someone to keep an eye on him.

Always tack up the youngster inside the horsebox; push aside the partitions and make yourself enough space to be able to do this. Then, when he comes down the ramp into the busy atmosphere of the show ground, he will be ready to ride and you won't be struggling to tack him up when he is excited.

I like to work in my young horse on the flat, just as I would at home, and then pop him over a couple of practice fences. I might also stand him in the collecting ring to watch the competition, and if I meet anyone I know, I will stop and chat to them so that he learns to stand still and relax. This is all part of the process of him learning good manners.

Be ready for your young horse to react to this new atmosphere. He may be excited, nervous and insecure, and you will need to be one step ahead of him. Be prepared for him to react to other horses working in around him by bucking or shooting forward. Sit securely

CHILLING OUT: As you prepare, chat with people and generally carry on as if you were getting ready to work at home

with your leg forward and be ready to push him on out of any naughtiness.

Make sure he has plenty of room, keep your distance from other competitors and be courteous to them – they, after all, have paid entry fees and have first refusal on working-in space and fences – and above all, try not to get yourself into a situation where you might get kicked, or kick someone else.

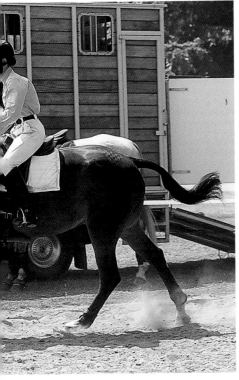

∨ **SIGHTS AND SOUNDS:** By the time he gets to his 'first' proper event, the young horse should be quite used to all the hustle and bustle of a showground

HOW THE COMPETITION STARTS AT HOME

Preparation is the key. Depending on what sort of first competition you are entering, you should have ridden the dressage test a few times in the preceding week – you must know the test so well yourself that it should be second nature, so that you can concentrate on riding it, rather than remembering it; and the horse should have jumped fences at home in training that are bigger and more difficult than the ones he will face in the competition.

Before a first showing class, the horse should have been worked in alongside other horses while visiting a show so that he is used to having other horses around him; he should be relaxed about standing still, and he should be used to being led in hand.

Before any of my horses take part in a one-day event, they will have spent time, probably during the previous winter, going to local indoor show-jumping shows. They will have learned to mix with other horses, to stand around in the collecting ring before it is their turn, to stop while I chat to people after my round, and, generally, to 'chill out'. They will have had the chance to take in all the sights and sounds of a show or an event before being really asked to work.

PREPARING YOURSELF

On the day of the competition, be sure to keep absolutely calm and composed yourself. Work out your own schedule for the day so you have plenty of time to pick up your number and get your horse and yourself ready. *You* don't want to be flustered too!

If the competition is affiliated (and even if it is not) make sure you are aware of the equipment, such as bits, and whips, that you are permitted to use. Don't leave it until you are at the showground to start fiddling with changes of tack.

Fit to compete

I find that the combination of hacking out – with the horse being ridden properly, not slopping along – plus flatwork and jumping sessions, will get a youngster quite fit enough for his first one-day event.

If I consider that a young horse feels particularly wobbly when asked to go faster during a cross-country school, I will take him for a session on the gallops to run alongside an older horse so that he learns to become more balanced and confident at speed; however, it isn't my usual practice.

Remember that it is the quality of the work which matters, not the quantity. There is no point spending hours trotting round in aimless circles which will only put wear and tear on a young horse's limbs and mentality, when you can achieve more, in half the time, by giving it proper work, in which it really uses itself.

Your young horse will naturally feel a bit unbalanced when he starts working at speed across country. Always ride him up to the bridle, so that he is working from the back end and making full use of his 'engine';

Just as with racehorses, competition horses do have different ground preferences. Primmore's Pride won his first three-day event in horrendous wet weather, and Supreme Rock was sixth at Badminton in 1999 in filthy weather. They are both mudlarks, but Walk On Star would much rather run on firm ground – whenever he went across country in wet, slippery or muddy conditions, he was pretty diffident about it. He was a classic case of a horse who needed to be sent hunting in winter to learn confidence in all types of ground conditions.

this applies to all paces. As he develops and becomes more powerful, so his back end will become stronger and his front end will lighten: he will come off his forehand, and this will place less strain on his front legs.

Think about the type of going you are riding on and reduce the strain on your horse's legs as much as possible. I prefer to give a five-year-old more work in the spring so that it can be turned away in summer. Endless runs on hard ground will surely take their toll later in your horse's life.

Hunting is a wonderful education for young horses. It provides a unique opportunity to teach a horse to work things out for itself: where to put its feet, how to cope with sudden changes of pace and trappy fences where no kind designer has built a groundline, and good manners – how to behave with other horses and to stand still.

Young Event Horse Classes

Do not work your horse so hard that by the time he has to perform he is tired, fed up and has lost the lift which says 'look at me'.

To work in for a young horse class, I would get on the horse about half an hour beforehand. If he felt a bit 'bright' I would canter him around for a few minutes, riding him forward out of any potential misbehaviour. Trying to get a horse to concentrate on flatwork while he is still buzzy and uptight is a mistake that many riders make, at all levels: it's a complete waste of time.

Some horses are better if you can spend 10-15 mins working quietly on the flat, then put them back in the lorry for 20 mins, then bring them out again to work in: they are often calmer the second time around.

Five minutes before you are due in the ring ask the horse to stand still on a loose rein while you check his tack and a helper – if you have one! – wipes him over. Pick him up, work him for a couple of minutes and then, bingo! In you go!

⋏ PRACTICE JUMPS: Only after 10 mins or so of working on the flat would I think about giving him a jump. I would start with taking a crosspole a couple of times, followed by once over a small vertical and then a bigger vertical and, finally, two or three times over an oxer. Again, it is a common mistake for riders to jump too much outside the ring. It is no good if he is being careless, and if he is being good it will only tire him unnecessarily

⋏ WORKING IN ON THE FLAT: Spend 10–15 minutes working him in quietly on the flat, in the same sort of routine as at home; try not to get flustered if he does not seem to be going as well as he does at home – if he is not used to working with other horses around he may find this unsettling. Ride quietly and firmly, and do not get into an argument with him because you are in a panic that he suddenly can't do something. It's just too late for that!

The Burghley Young Event Horse competition has qualifiers that take place all around the country at events and shows and offers an excellent introductory competition for a young horse, whether its future is in eventing or not. For someone like me, who is busy with older horses during the eventing season, it is an incentive to get a four-year-old horse prepared and out for a competition.

The class is judged on a horse's type and potential for eventing. I have had some wonderful horses to ride in this series, including Jurassic Rising and Midnight Magic, who both won the four-year-old finals, and Mythical Rising, Cavalcade, Primmore's Pride and Designer Tramp, winners of the five-year-old championship. All these horses have, so far, gone on and made very successful event horses – some have won three-day events.

⋀ **BURGHLEY YOUNG EVENT HORSE WINNER:** Midnight Magic, who won the final as a four-year-old, has a wonderful, bold approach to life and is now successfully competing at four-star level in Canada

These horses were all quality animals in their own right, but presentation is important for success in this type of competition. Often you see super young horses being ridden sloppily and way below their potential, while competent riders will maximise the good points in really quite average horses. A large part of any showing or dressage-based competition is the art of presenting your horse in such a way as to make the judges' heads turn.

PRESENTING YOUR YOUNG HORSE

When you get in the ring, sit up and ride the horse as if you feel you're on the best in the class. Ride the dressage test, which is generally the first part, as accurately as you can. A four-year-old won't be balanced and strong enough to go deep into corners, and it might be suspicious of the surrounding white boards which it may not have seen before, so don't get into a battle about exactly where he puts his feet, and instead aim for a smooth, flowing, forward-moving test.

What you are aiming for – and what the judges are looking for – is for the horse to stay submissive to the aids while going forward in a balanced manner. The test is not marked on individual movements; it is marked on the judge's impression of the whole picture.

The jumping phase follows immediately, so make it clear to the horse that you're now in 'jump mode', a new section. This also applies to the show-jumping phase of a one-day event. Gather the horse together, get it into a brisk forward canter and ride in between fences so that it understands what task is coming next. Be particularly aware of riding positively towards the first fence so that the horse wakes up and realises what it has to do. Try and keep in a good rhythm between fences, as this will show off your horse's jump better and give it more chance of jumping well.

For the conformation judging and leading in hand, you will need a helper to remove the saddle and boots and help wipe the horse down. As stated previously, it is important to have taught a horse to lead properly: he should move naturally alongside you, with you moving level with his shoulder. Nothing looks worse than a horse which either has to be dragged, or one which gets ahead of its leader so that its head is being pulled around. This will prevent the horse's movement being shown off, and it can even make it look lame.

If all has gone well, your young horse will be pulled into the final judging. This is like a showing class, and success in this discipline is an art of its own, involving a certain amount of common sense and ring craft on the part of the rider. For instance, if your horse is a little short of showy movement, don't get behind another horse which has particularly elastic, athletic paces because it will only highlight your own horse's shortcomings!

Give your horse plenty of space – don't sit on the tail of the one in front – and use the whole of the ring. Don't try to be clever by cutting

GOING FOR THE GALLOP!: (*above*) You have to be brave when it comes for the gallop, but you will only be asking your horse to gallop for 10-20 strides. If he cannot cope with this kind of distance, then he will not really be any good for a competitive career

WINNING COMBINATION: (*right*) Denise and Roger Lincoln's Midnight Magic, after having won the four-year old final in 1997. All the horses who have won either the four- or five-year-old finals have gone on to achieve considerable success as event horses

into the centre. Keep an eye on the judges and the direction of their glances: when they're not looking at you, you can relax a little, but when you know you've got their attention, sit up, ride forward and show off your horse's stride.

When it comes to the gallop, you just have to be brave! It depresses me to see people who are not prepared to go for it here. Gather the horse together and set him up to gallop before you get to the long side of the arena, so that you are ready to come out of the corner with the horse balanced and his energy coming from his back end, rather than being on the forehand. Give yourself plenty of room – the judges won't mind if you turn a circle to gain more space – and don't gallop up the backside of the horse in front. Sit securely in case he feels like putting in an exuberant buck! It is also equally important to be ready to slow down at the other end of the ring! Be ready to sit quietly and pat him.

I often hear people saying 'I'm not galloping my horse on that hard ground', but you're only talking about 10-20 strides and if a horse can't handle that short distance at gallop, there's no hope of it standing up to a real competitive career. And it's always the same people who complain about the going at shows who then turn their horse out that evening to buck and canter around on equally hard ground!

The first event

When you know your riding times, plan backwards accordingly: you need time to walk the cross-country course, looking for all the alternative routes at combination fences in case you need them, time to get yourself and the horse dressed, and time to warm up for your dressage test.

I rarely work a horse for more than half an hour before the dressage unless I think it is going to be particularly lively, in which case I might allow time for a 20-minute lungeing session. Do not expect a horse to perform at its best if it has been ridden for an hour or more beforehand.

At three-day events many riders, even experienced ones, make the mistake of overdoing the flatwork, with two or three sessions a day. I have found it is better to vary the work – a flatwork session, some lungeing and a hack. Overdoing flatwork will only make the horse more tense. If the training has been done correctly at home, the horse will know that it is expected to become submissive within a short time.

⋏ **ENTERING THE ARENA:** Matter of Fact (Matty) at one of his first novice one-day events at Smith's Lawn

THE DRESSAGE TEST

Rider nerves often spoil a dressage test. Horses are sensitive and they will pick up on the rider's tenseness: once the rider's leg comes off the horse through nerves, he will become lit up and tense himself. It's easier said than done, but try and ride as you would at home – relax, enjoy, and go into the arena with the attitude 'hey, look at my horse!'

I was once given a horse to ride which had a serious problem with blowing up when it got into a dressage arena. It had clearly been hassled and 'got after' by its previous rider and had begun to associate the competition arena with a bad experience.

On our first competition outing together he became so uptight during the test that I brought him back to a walk, patted him and told him to relax. We somehow got through the test and, after the final halt, instead of leaving the arena on a long rein, I did several circles and loops, getting him to relax. I think the judge thought I was mad! Then, having left the arena, I let him pick some grass and made a huge fuss of him, letting him know I was pleased with him.

He soon realised that he wasn't going to be punished for the way he had gone and his very next test was 75 percent better. By the third test, he would allow me to ride him and was relaxed. This horse naturally found dressage difficult because he did not have a good conformation for it; he was also very sensitive, and I realised that I had to ride him more sympathetically. He was, of course, an unusual and exaggerated case, but as a general rule, if the rider stays relaxed in their mind and rides in competition as they would at home, there is far less risk of this sort of problem. Horses tend to 'blow up' in the dressage arena not because they're difficult, but because their preparation has been wrong – the daily routine has not been consistent enough, or the rider isn't sitting straight. These shortcomings will all work against you at a competition.

⋏ **RIDING THE TEST:** In this picture, I have just come across the diagonal in canter, changed legs through trot at X and struck off on the left leg. As you can see from Matty's expression there was some resistance in the transition.

Don't throw away silly marks; instead, your attitude should be "what marks can I steal?" If the test instructs you to "canter at A", then canter exactly at A, not a stride before or two strides later. In this way, even if the horse is not going as well as you might have hoped, you won't throw away marks. If you do make an error – the wrong strike-off, a break in pace – don't panic. It's happened, so take the attitude 'right, now I've got to get those marks back'

⋗ **CORRECTING A RAGGED HALT:** Trot to halt is a very difficult transition for a young horse, so you may need to allow a couple of strides of walk before the halt. Here Matty has made a rather wobbly halt, he is still quite immature and finds it hard to engage his quarters, as a result his legs are all over the place at first. By quietly nudging him on, I've tidied up his straggled stance, but as I acknowledge the judge at the end of the test, you can see that Matty is rather overbent. I have held on to the contact to prevent him shuffling forward and losing marks, but this has made him lower his head somewhat. Finally, it's important to reward the horse, no matter what kind of test he's done, because he must relate working in the arena to happy experiences

THE SHOWJUMPING ROUND

The show jumping phase for event riders is often the weakest and does need time spending on it. But whether your ambition lies in eventing or show jumping the art is to keep that good quality canter, where the horse is carrying himself without you having him too pressured between the hand and leg. This should have been worked on at home so that it is already established before he goes into the ring for the first time. Remember, the less the rider interferes the better chance the horse has of jumping the fence clear.

Be sure you know the course thoroughly having walked it earlier and that you are aware of all the distances. Try and make time to watch some fellow competitors, you can learn so much from watching other riders of all levels of experience. When you are happy that you know the course, and happy about how your horse has jumped while you worked him in, you are ready to go.

With the young horse I will canter positively into the ring and then usually bring him back to a walk. If I have the chance I will let him look at one or two fences, but not in a manner that makes it obvious to the judge. Then as soon as the bell goes I will go forward into a good quality canter and try to maintain a consistent rhythm, rather than interfering and worrying what stride I am on. I am constantly aware that I am riding a young one, ready to back him up with my legs in case he suddenly spooks at a fence or perhaps gets distracted by any of the arena spectators. At the end of the round don't just collapse in a heap: I try to end in a balanced manner by circling and making correct transitions back to walk. Above all don't forget to reward your horse whatever his performance was like.

▽ **THE SECOND PHASE:** Matty clearing a double in the show jumping phase at Smith's Lawn in 2001. He makes a lovely shape over the first element of a double (*top left*), but lands a bit short (*top right*), so I have to react quickly to make up the ground so he can get the correct single stride in (*bottom left*). I should have done this with a more upright body – I am slightly in front of the movement (*bottom centre*) due to not being quick enough to sit up between the elements. Despite this Matty clears the fence (*bottom right*) and goes on to jump a clear round

TROUBLESHOOTING

What if my horse has a lot of show jumps down?

There are a number of possible causes of this. Very often a lack of rhythm is the root of the problem – maybe you have approached a fence too quickly and not given him time to jump or maybe you have not had sufficient impulsion. Did you approach the fence straight or did you cut the corner, or overshoot the corner so the horse was unable to come balanced off the fence? Whatever the reason, it is important to analyse what happened so that you know what to work on at home. It is worth remembering that some horses are not as careful as others and will need certain exercises at home to help them improve their technique and concentrate on the jumps more (see pages 92-3). Do not be tempted to interfere too much with the slightly careless youngster, let him learn by his own mistakes.

What if my horse keeps stopping?

Stopping is more often than not due to a lack of confidence. A careful horse is more likely to stop than a bold one, so the more timid sort will obviously need to do a lot more jumping at home to build up their confidence. A naturally bold horse will jump from whatever spot he arrives at a fence, even if that means crashing through it, but even those will eventually lose heart if they are constantly having to bust a gut to get out of trouble. If your youngster refuses regularly it is important to have rhythm and impulsion, but also to make extra sure the horse is in front of the leg. Do not be tempted to use speed as a means to get a horse over its fences. I am not against giving a sharp kick or a quick smack but it must be done straightaway, not 5 or 10 seconds later, so that he realises that this kind of disobedience will not be tolerated.

THE CROSS-COUNTRY PHASE

One of the secrets of successful cross-country riding is the ability to adapt to surprise situations. This is even more important when riding the novice horse across country.

When you walk the cross-country course, look at the going and where it might be slippery or rough, look at the things which may distract the horse and cause him to lose concentration – this will be the first time your youngster has seen fence judges, people walking the course, flags, sponsor's boards and so on – and be aware of all the alternative options at fences. Even if you are planning to take the direct route – and the horse should be sufficiently well prepared for you to do so – something may happen during your round which causes you to change your mind quickly. The horse may have made an awkward jump at the previous fence and need its confidence restoring; it may have frightened itself at a water complex and need a quieter approach next time. You will know when you have perhaps been a bit lucky to get away with a mistake, so don't push your luck at the next fence.

⋟ INTO THE WATER: Matty jumping his first proper-sized fence into the water at Smith's Lawn. I'm glad to say his facial expression is more confident than mine!

⋏ IN THE START BOX: Best of All (Muffin) quietly waiting before his round

⋞ ON THE COURSE: Always make sure your horse is warmed-up. Here I am quietly popping Muffin over the practice jump, without any pressure

If a horse slips as he goes across country he may lose his nerve, so minimise the chances of that happening by wearing the appropriate studs – and allow enough time to put these in. I always go across country with studs in, but I only put one stud in each of the hind shoes, on the outside, because I am nervous of the horse striking into himself. I usually only put one stud in the outside of the front shoes also, unless it is very slippery going, in which case I might put a smaller rounded stud on the inside of the hoof. Not everyone would agree with me, suggesting that the foot is not balanced with only one stud: it is a personal choice.

I personally tend to look at one-day events as a training ground for the ultimate test of three-day eventing, but no one, whatever their reason for eventing, should think they are necessarily going to win first time out by going inside the time.

Both Primmore's Pride and Teddy Twilight were notorious spookers who, as youngsters, looked at everything else except the fences. I despaired of Teddy in particular, who was always finding a reason to be naughty, and I was slightly amazed when he won his first three-day event, as a seven-year-old. With horses like that, you have to ride with even more determination, keeping your leg on and thinking ahead all the time.

Ride forward strongly and keep the horse in front of the leg, but always allow the young horse time to see the cross-country fences. The objective is to have an enjoyable, calm round, keeping the horse balanced and moving forward. Trying to achieve the optimum time doesn't come into the equation; the aim is to build up the horse's confidence and assess how successful his training and preparation have been.

Remember that no matter how thorough your cross-country training has been, on this first competitive outing your youngster may suddenly spot the fence judge's picnic five strides away from the fence and you will find yourself facing in a completely different direction! And on some of the more wooded type of cross-country track, where there is no view, you may come whizzing around a corner to find someone walking the course in a bright anorak with a dog!

⩗ **TACKLING A SPREAD:** Muffin approaching the second fence at Smith's Lawn. It is vitally important to be positive over the first few fences of a course. You need plenty of impulsion, getting your horse in front of your leg, but you are not aiming for more speed

Partnership

 The over-riding theme I have tried to impart in this book is that producing a young horse is all about building up a bond of trust, so that as each stage of development is approached, the horse never feels that the rider is asking him to do something which is frightening, too difficult or for which he is not sufficiently prepared.

For this reason, no one else schools my horses apart from myself. This is not because my staff are not competent to do so – in fact they are a great team – it is because of my strong belief that it is the building up of a partnership with a horse which is the single most important factor for success. Also, it would make me very lazy!

Horses are intelligent, generous and usually long to please. They are also strong, unpredictable, easily unnerved and frustrating. Huge reserves of time and patience are needed to train a horse. But when the perseverance pays off and the system I have learned, stuck to and found to work produces its rewards, there is nothing more satisfying. Equally, it is important to realise when a horse really isn't going to be suitable for his intended job – in my case, if he isn't brave enough for cross-country – and acknowledge that he would be much happier in a different career.

Thanks to some wonderful support from others, I have been lucky enough to enjoy some wonderful results at top level, but it can be just as thrilling when a young horse shows that he has learned something. There is no expectation in the early stages of a horse's career, so every time he goes well it is a bonus.

When I was younger, I was so very competitive and impatient to win. The hunger for success is certainly still with me at major competitions, but lower down the grades I have realised that how a horse goes means more than the colour of his rosette. I also remain self-critical after every phase at every competition on every horse. Where could I have improved? No rider ever stops learning, and the day they think they have is the day their standards will drop.

However much help I have had from parents, friends, sponsors and trainers, especially Ruth McMullen, I still find that the most influential trainers are the horses themselves.

THE HARD WORK PAYS OFF: With luck, many of the youngsters in this book will give as much pleasure and success as these three older boys hacking to the gallop. Kate Flatley on Paddy (left), Zanie Tanswell on Charlie (centre) and myself on Rocky

Index

ACKNOWLEDGEMENTS

There have been so many people throughout my riding career that have been so influential or who have helped and supported me through the highs and lows of my life with horses. I am just one part of a very large team.

Over the last twelve years William has given me help with so many horses and is great to bounce ideas off – to have a husband who is a top class show jumper is a huge bonus! I also couldn't have achieved what I have without all the support my parents have given me over the years.

Ruth McMullen gave me the opportunity to follow my dreams from an early age and I wouldn't like to add up the number of hours of help she has given me over the years. It was this help that instilled in me the importance of patience, straightness and balance, and working with your horse, not against it.

I'd also like to thank the owners who have given me the chance to ride some wonderful horse over the years: Sarah and Richard Jewson, Janet and Ian McIntyre, Emma Pitt, Denise and Roger Lincoln (who have bred Primmore's Patriot, featured in chapter 3), Susie Cranston, Sue Bunn, Barbara and Nick Walkinshaw, Ann Burnet and Jane and Andy Croft.

My thanks too to the following:

Becky Coffey, who is a distant relative, comes to every event and is an invaluable supporter, as well as having the unenviable job of sorting out most of my entries!

My stable girls, Zanie Tanswell and Lucy Turner, as well as Nini French, who left last year after six years with me. These girls work very hard and are often the unsung heroes. The love, care and dedication they give to the horses is a credit to them all.

My sponsors who have supported me throughout the years: Equine America, Toggi and British Equestrian Insurance Brokers.
I look forward to my involvement with Devoucoux, Woof Ware, Virbac, Horseware and Champion in the coming year.

The final, most important acknowledgment must go …

TO THE HORSES

A DAVID & CHARLES BOOK

All photography by Kit Houghton except the following:

Author's collection pp 11(btm left), 17(top)
Iain Burns p18
Shaw Shot pp 10, 145(right)

Additional text by Anne Plume on page 34, and within some troubleshooting sections

Commissioning editor Jane Trollope
Art editor Sue Cleave
Desk editor Tom McCann
Project editor Anne Plume

First published in the UK in 2002

A catalogue record for this book is available from the British Library.

ISBN 0 7153 1207 3

Printed in Singapore by KHL
for David & Charles
Brunel House   Newton Abbot   Devon